JAMES McNAIR's
SOUPS

Photography by Patricia Brabant

Chronicle Books • San Francisco

Printed in Japan

Library of Congress
Cataloging-in-Publication Data
McNair, James K.
 [Soups]
 James McNair's Soups/
 photography by Patricia Brabant.
  p. cm.
 Includes index.
 ISBN 0-87701-761-1.
 ISBN 0-87701-753-0 (pbk.)
 1. Soups. I. Title.
TX757.M43 1990
641.8'13—dc20   90-2222
                         CIP

Distributed in Canada by
Raincoast Books
112 East Third Avenue
Vancouver, British Columbia V5T 1C8

10 9 8 7 6 5 4 3

Chronicle Books
275 Fifth Street
San Francisco, California 94103

For Mark Leno, a wonderful friend who has been extremely supportive and encouraging throughout the production of this book series. It is comforting to know that he is always there for me.

And in memory of Douglas Jackson, who was one of the kindest men and gentlest souls with whom I have shared this life.

Produced by The Rockpile Press, San Francisco and Lake Tahoe

Art direction, photographic and food styling, and book design by James McNair

Editorial production assistance by Lin Cotton

Editorial and styling assistance by Ellen Berger-Quan

Photography assistance by M. J. Murphy

Typography and mechanical production by Cleve Gallat and Charles N. Sublett of CTA Graphics

CONTENTS

COMFORT, NUTRITION, & FLAVOR

Most of us have memories of steaming bowls of soup that warmed the cockles of our hearts when we were ill. For some, it's chicken soup, affectionately dubbed "Jewish penicillin;" for me, it's tomato, a soup I will probably always associate with my mother, bed trays, and the security of simpler days.

Throughout our lives, we've been admonished to eat our soup because it was good for us. Nutritionists wholeheartedly agree with such motherly advice. Indeed, a bowl of broth, bouillon, consommé, chowder, porridge, bisque, or any other kind of soup is usually chock-full of nutrients, but the intent of this book is to celebrate the varied great tastes of these perennial favorites.

When an old friend heard that I was working on a volume of soups, he mentioned that soup around his house always meant a chance to clean out the refrigerator. Unfortunately, such frugality is an accepted practice. Since any dish simply cannot turn out better than the ingredients from which it is made, however, a truly memorable bowl of soup starts with the finest and freshest ingredients available—from stock to garnish.

After a few brief tips on how to improve the quality of soups coming from your kitchen, along with basic recipes for well-flavored stocks, I've divided the recipes into three sections. VEGETABLE SOUPS, arranged from spring through winter, take advantage of seasonal produce. Although many of the vegetable soups include meat-based stock or broth and dairy products, strict vegetarians can adapt these by preparing a flavorful vegetable stock and substituting soy products for milk, cream, or cheese, or thickening the soup with a little cornstarch. FISH, POULTRY, & MEAT SOUPS contain both ethnic recipes and old favorites to perk up any soup repertoire. The section on FRUIT & NUT SOUPS includes recipes to start, interrupt, or end a meal with unexpected flavor and elegance.

SOUP AND THE DIET

According to a study published by University of Pennsylvania researchers, soup consumed at the beginning of a meal slows the rate of eating. It fills the stomach, which signals the brain to curtail the appetite. As a result, less calories are consumed during the meal.

When soups that call for heavy cream don't fit into your diet, use half-and-half, whole milk, or low-fat milk, or thicken the soup with puréed cooked rice or potato. In place of melting rich cheeses into simmering soups, use reduced-fat cream cheese or soybean curd. Instead of dollops of sour cream or crème fraîche, top off with low-fat plain yogurt.

COOKING

It is impossible to overstress the importance of starting with ingredients that are of the highest quality and impeccably fresh; leftovers are fine to add to soups as long as they meet such criteria.

To add depth to the flavor of some soups, I often suggest sautéing some of the vegetables before adding liquid. Although it is quite possible to make decent soup with only water as the liquid, the use of stocks, broths, juices, or dairy products will add to the range of flavors.

For soups containing cream or cheese, it is generally best to add the dairy product shortly before serving. The soup can be prepared a couple of days ahead up to this point. Boiled cream soups or those with cheese may curdle or separate, so cook over low heat and watch carefully.

Microwave ovens can be used quite successfully for most soups. Space prohibits me from adding microwave directions to each recipe, but a basic microwave cookbook will give you general guidelines for adapting my conventional recipes to microwaves. I highly recommend the superb volumes by Barbara Kafka.

STORING

Many soups taste much better the second or third day, after the flavors meld. In the recipes, I've indicated those that should be served immediately after preparing. Chilling meat-based soups also provides a chance to easily remove any excess fat before reheating.

Tight-sealing plastic, glass, or ceramic containers are best for storing soups. Avoid those made of tin, iron, copper, or other reactive materials that might impart a metallic taste.

Some soups will thicken as they chill. To be served cold, they may need to be thinned by whisking in some additional liquid. Use the same stock or broth, water, light or heavy cream, milk, or vegetable juice that was used to make the soup.

Most soups can be frozen for longer storage. Before placing it in the freezer, cool the soup completely in the refrigerator, then transfer it to tight-sealing freezer containers that will hold the amount of soup you will want to serve at one time. Thaw and slowly reheat to avoid overcooking ingredients.

REHEATING

Soups containing cream or cheese must be reheated very slowly over low heat; a double boiler works well, as does a microwave oven. No matter what the reheating method, stir the soup quite frequently and avoid boiling, which will curdle the cream and separate cheese.

SERVING

Many of the soups in this volume may be served either piping hot or chilled. When presented cold, more seasoning may be needed than would be used in hot soup. Taste before ladling and adjust the seasonings as desired. With a few exceptions, chilled soups taste best when removed from the refrigerator about 20 minutes before serving.

When serving soup hot, it is desirable to preheat bowls or tureens in a low oven and reheat the soup just prior to ladling. Conversely, well-chilled bowls from the refrigerator or freezer are a nice touch for cold soups.

Wide-rimmed shallow bowls are the most elegant containers for soup, although for fun you might want to serve soup in mugs, goblets, ice cream dishes, or other fanciful containers. When serving hot soup in glass containers, be sure the dishes are made of heat-resistant tempered glass.

GARNISHING

The photos and recipes in this book are filled with suggestions for finishing off a bowl of soup. Additionally, consider the following:

Fresh herb sprigs or leaves
Chiffonnade (long shreds) of
    leafy greens or herbs
Whole peas, asparagus tips,
    tomato slices
Julienne-cut leeks, carrots,
    sweet peppers, or snow peas
Cubed avocado or bean curd (tofu)
Chopped or sliced olives
Slivered or minced citrus zest
Sliced or wedged fruits
Cooked small dumplings, ravioli,
    quenelles, or gnocchi
Pesticide-free non-toxic flowers
Grated cheese
Crème fraîche, sour cream, yogurt,
    whipped cream, or mayonnaise
    (plain or flavored with garlic,
    saffron, or tomato paste)
Drizzles of pesto or salsa
Dollops of caviar
Croutons, toasted bread, cheese toast,
    interesting crackers
Toasted nuts or seeds
Thinly sliced or minced truffle
Crumbled cooked bacon or pancetta
Slivered prosciutto or other ham
Sliced sausage, salami, pepperoni
Cooked whole shrimp

CANNED BROTH

Although flavorful homemade stocks are the most desirable base for soups, canned broths make quite acceptable substitutes. Try to locate low-salt or unsalted versions in order to have more control over the seasoning. If canned broth proves too salty, dilute it with a liquid that is complementary to the other ingredients: water, vegetable or fruit juice, milk, or wine.

To enrich canned broths, in a saucepan combine about 4 cups broth with a chopped onion, a chopped carrot, a chopped celery stalk, some peppercorns, some fresh herbs, and perhaps some fresh ginger and garlic. Bring to a boil, then reduce the heat to low, cover, and simmer for 35 to 45 minutes. Strain the broth into a container and discard the vegetables and herbs.

FLAVORFUL STOCKS

Soup-making can be a breeze when a good ready-to-use stock is on hand. To assure this possibility, make favorite stocks in quantity and store in the refrigerator or freezer. Or keep several cans of broths on hand for quick and easy soups.

Stock is derived from simmering meat and bones of poultry, meat, game, or fish with aromatic vegetables. Members of the onion family are essential to good stock; other vegetables round out and vary the flavor. Keep in mind that soups calling for stock will turn out no better than the stock with which you start, so always use the highest quality and freshest ingredients available. Making stock is not the time to clean the refrigerator of ingredients that are past their prime.

Tough cuts of meat, trimmings, and bones render flavorful stock. Throw trimmings into a freezer bag and save until you have enough to make stock.

Poultry stock made with chicken is probably the one most frequently used in soups. Although gizzards, hearts, and necks add richness to the stock, discard livers or save them for another purpose; they make an off-flavored, cloudy stock.

Since bacteria can rapidly grow in stock left at room temperature for too long, and tightly covered warm stock placed in the refrigerator can sour or ferment, I suggest cooling finished stock as quickly as possible, uncovered, in the refrigerator. If time allows, chill the stock completely before using. Not only will the flavors meld, but excess fat will rise to the surface and congeal, making removal easy. If you need to use the stock before cooling it, refrigerate it for about 10 minutes, then carefully skim off the surface fat with a fine-mesh metal skimmer, slotted utensil, or wire strainer.

After cooling, store stock in tight-sealing containers of plastic, glass, or stainless steel; stocks stored in uncoated aluminum, copper, iron, or tin containers will take on a metallic taste. Except for fish stock, which should be used within 2 days, stock can be refrigerated for up to 5 days; this time period can be extended by boiling the stock for a few minutes, then cooling and storing it as before. For longer storage, freeze the stock as soon as it is cooled. Whether it is taken from the refrigerator or the freezer, always reheat stock to boiling before using.

Contrary to suggestions in many cookbooks, I don't advise saving the meat from stocks for other purposes; the flavor and nutrients are all cooked out. I pick over the remains and add the bits of meat to pet food.

For a more concentrated stock, boil the strained and cooled stock until it is reduced to about one third the original volume. Cool, uncovered, in the refrigerator, then pour it into ice cube trays and freeze until solid. Transfer frozen stock cubes to a plastic freezer bag. Combine thawed cubes with water to reconstitute the stock to desired strength.

Use the recipes on the following four pages as guides for making your own stocks, adding seasonal vegetables for variety.

CONSOMMÉ OR BOUILLON

For an elegant beginning to a special meal, serve a flavorful stock that has been clarified to remove all particles of fat.

Prepare 2 quarts stock. Chill thoroughly and remove any fat that rises to the surface.

In a large pot, beat 1 cup egg whites (from 3 or 4 large eggs) with a wire whisk until frothy. Whisk in the crushed shells from the eggs and the stock. Place over medium-low heat, beating constantly to keep the egg whites from solidifying, until the mixture comes to a gentle boil. Reduce the heat to low and simmer, stirring frequently, until the egg whites have absorbed all the fat and tiny particles from the stock, about 35 to 45 minutes.

Strain the clear stock into a bowl through a colander or sieve lined with several layers of dampened cheesecloth. For an exceptionally clear stock, repeat the procedure.

Use immediately, or cool slightly, cover, and refrigerate for up to 3 days. Reheat before serving. Ladle over vegetables that have been cut into julienne or fanciful shapes, then briefly blanched or steamed.

Poultry Stock

4 to 5 pounds chicken, duck, turkey,
    or other poultry bones, with
    some meat attached, including
    necks, backs, wings, gizzards,
    and hearts (do not add liver)
4 quarts cold water
4 large unpeeled carrots,
    cut into 3-inch lengths
2 celery stalks, including leaves,
    cut into 3-inch lengths
2 large unpeeled onions,
    cut into thick slices
2 whole leeks, split lengthwise, rinsed,
    and cut into 3-inch lengths
4 unpeeled garlic cloves, smashed
4 or 5 fresh parsley sprigs
2 or 3 fresh thyme sprigs, or
    1 tablespoon crumbled
    dried thyme
2 or 3 bay leaves
About 1 teaspoon black peppercorns
Salt

Chicken stock is the most commonly used soup base. For the sake of variety, try stock made from other fowl.

Quickly rinse the poultry bones and parts under cold running water. Place on a cutting surface and cut off and discard excess fat. Whack the poultry into small pieces with a heavy cleaver. Transfer to a stockpot, add water, and bring to a boil over medium heat. Using a slotted or wire utensil, skim to remove any foamy scum that rises to the surface.

Add the carrots, celery, onions, leeks, garlic, parsley, thyme, bay leaves, peppercorns and salt to taste. Bring to a boil, reduce the heat to low, cover, and simmer for 4 to 5 hours; skim off the foam as necessary during the early stages of cooking, but do not stir. Remove from heat and cool for a few minutes.

Strain the stock into a large bowl through a colander or sieve lined with several layers of dampened cheesecloth, pressing the vegetables to release all liquid. Discard the poultry, vegetables, and herbs. Refrigerate the warm stock, uncovered, until cold. Remove any fat that rises and solidifies on the surface. Reheat the stock and use immediately, or cover and refrigerate for up to 4 days, or freeze for up to 6 months. Reheat to boiling before using.

Makes about 2 to 3 quarts.

ASIAN VARIATION Omit the vegetables and herbs. Add 8 thin slices unpeeled fresh ginger root and 4 green onions, including the green tops, cut into 3-inch lengths. Substitute Sichuan peppercorns for the black ones.

Meat Stock

Whether you choose beef, veal, lamb, pork, or game, meat stocks are more flavorful when the bones and meat are browned before adding liquid. For a light stock, use bones that have some meat attached. For a richer stock, add a chunk of meat.

Preheat an oven to 450° F.

Quickly rinse the bones and meat (if using) under cold running water. Place on a cutting surface and cut off and discard excess fat. Toss the bones, meat, and onions in the oil. Spread in a baking pan and roast in the oven, turning frequently, until lightly browned, about 50 minutes. Transfer to a stockpot.

Add enough cold water to the stockpot to cover the ingredients. Bring to a boil over high heat. Reduce the heat to low and simmer for about 6 minutes. Drain and discard the liquid and rinse the bones, meat, and onions under running cold water. Drain again. Rinse the stockpot and add the drained bones, meat, and onions.

Add all the remaining ingredients, including salt to taste. Bring to a boil over medium-high heat. Reduce the heat to low and simmer, partially covered, until the stock is richly flavored, 5 to 8 hours. Use a slotted or wire utensil to skim the surface to remove any foamy scum during the early stages of cooking; do not stir. During the last hour of cooking, add salt to taste and remove the cover. Remove from heat and cool for a few minutes.

Strain the stock into a large bowl through a colander or sieve lined with several layers of dampened cheesecloth, pressing the vegetables to release all liquid. Discard the bones, meat, vegetables, and herbs. Refrigerate the warm stock, uncovered, until cold. Remove any fat that rises and solidifies on the surface. Reheat the stock and use immediately, or cover and refrigerate for up to 4 days, or freeze for up to 6 months. Reheat to boiling before using.

Makes about 2 to 3 quarts.

3 pounds bones such as shin, shank, short rib, neck, knuckle, or oxtail, with some meat attached (saw large bones crosswise into 3-inch pieces)
2 pounds meat (optional)
2 large unpeeled yellow onions, thickly sliced
3 tablespoons vegetable oil
3 celery stalks, cut into 3-inch lengths
3 large unpeeled carrots, cut into 3-inch lengths
1 whole large leek, split lengthwise, rinsed, and cut into 3-inch lengths
2 large unpeeled parsnips, cut into 3-inch pieces
2 large turnips, quartered
4 or 5 sprigs fresh parsley sprigs, preferably flat-leaf type
4 or 5 fresh thyme sprigs
2 bay leaves
About 1 teaspoon black peppercorns
4 quarts water
Salt

Fish Stock (Fumet)

3 pounds heads, bones, and
    trimmings from white-fleshed
    fish
2 medium-sized unpeeled
    yellow onions, thickly sliced
2 whole large leeks, split lengthwise,
    rinsed, and cut into 3-inch
    lengths
2 celery stalks, including leaves,
    cut into 3-inch lengths
4 or 5 fresh parsley sprigs
2 bay leaves
2 or 3 fresh tarragon or thyme sprigs,
    or 1 teaspoon crumbled dried
    tarragon or thyme
Zest from 1 lemon
About ½ teaspoon white peppercorns
4 cups dry white wine
4 cups water
Salt

Avoid oily fish such as salmon or mackerel. Toss in shells from lobster or shrimp, if available.

Wash the fish bones and parts under cold running water. Crack the fish heads and place all the fish parts in a stockpot. Add the onions, leeks, celery, parsley, bay leaves, tarragon or thyme, lemon zest, and peppercorns. Add the wine and water. Bring to a boil over medium-high heat, then reduce the heat to low and simmer, uncovered, for 45 minutes to 1 hour. Use a slotted or wire utensil to remove any foamy scum that comes to the surface during cooking; do not stir. Season to taste with salt.

Strain the stock into a large bowl through a colander or sieve lined with several layers of dampened cheesecloth; discard the fish, vegetables, and herbs. Use immediately, or refrigerate, uncovered, until cold, then tightly cover and store up to 2 days, or freeze for up to 3 months. Reheat to boiling before using.

Makes about 2 quarts.

Vegetable Stock

Add ingredients according to seasonal availability, taste, and how you plan to use the stock. It is generally best not to mix strongly flavored vegetables such as asparagus or broccoli, or to use intensely colored vegetables such as beets. Although they add good flavor to stock, potatoes will render stock cloudy. Choose herbs that will blend well with the soup in which the stock will be used.

Place all the ingredients, except salt, in a large stockpot, add water, and bring to a boil over medium heat. Using a slotted or wire utensil, skim to remove any foam that rises to the surface. Reduce the heat to low, cover, and simmer for 4 to 5 hours, skimming as necessary but never stirring. Remove from heat and cool for a few minutes. Season to taste with salt.

Strain the stock into a large bowl through a colander or sieve lined with several layers of dampened cheesecloth, pressing the vegetables to release all liquid. Discard the vegetables and herbs. Rinse the pot, pour in the strained stock, and bring to a gentle boil over medium heat. Cook until reduced to about 2 quarts, about 1 to 1½ hours. Remove from heat and use immediately or let stand until cold. Cover tightly and chill for up to 4 days, or freeze for up to 6 months; reheat to boiling before using.

Makes about 2 quarts.

4 large unpeeled yellow or white
    onions, thickly sliced
2 large whole leeks, split lengthwise,
    rinsed, and cut into 3-inch
    lengths
2 or 3 unpeeled garlic cloves, smashed
6 large unpeeled carrots,
    cut into 3-inch lengths
6 celery stalks, including leaves,
    cut into 3-inch lengths
2 bay leaves
About 6 fresh herb sprigs
1 teaspoon black peppercorns
4 quarts water
Salt

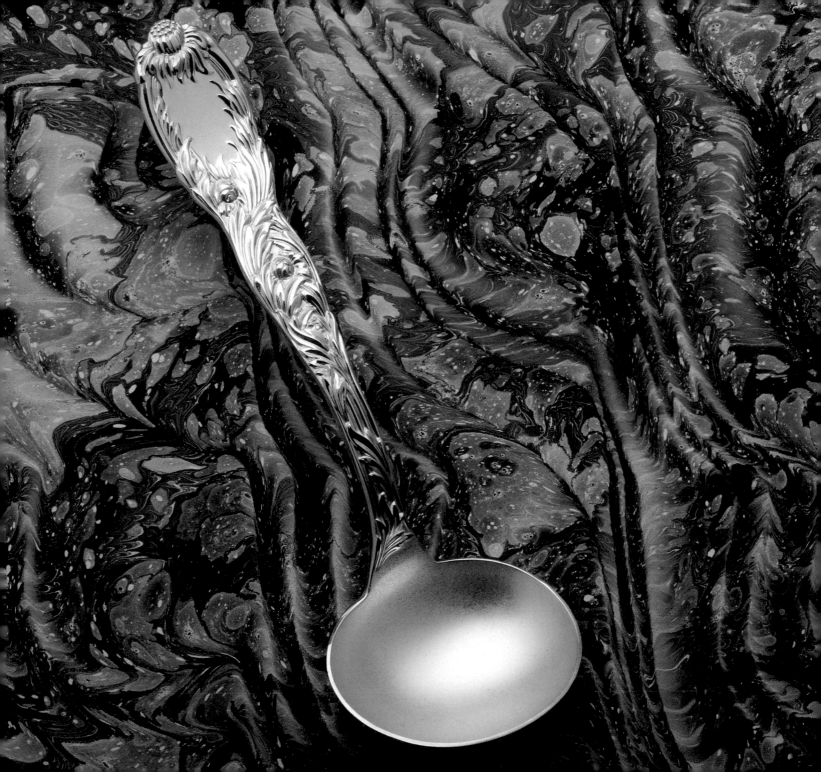

Vegetable Soups

Cream of Almost-Any-Vegetable Soup

½ cup (1 stick) unsalted butter,
  olive oil, or safflower or other
  high-quality vegetable oil
2 cups chopped onion or leek,
  including pale green portion of
  leek
2 pounds asparagus or other raw
  vegetable, trimmed and cut into
  small pieces
3 cups Vegetable Stock (page 13),
  Poultry Stock (page 10), or
  canned chicken broth,
  preferably low-salt type
1 cup heavy (whipping) cream
Salt
Freshly ground white pepper
Sliced blanched asparagus or
  fresh herb sprigs for garnish
Pesticide-free, non-toxic flowers such
  as lilac for garnish (optional)

Although I've chosen asparagus for the recipe and photo, you may vary this basic recipe by substituting almost any vegetable at its peak of flavor. Sauté garlic to taste along with the onion when the flavor seems compatible with the selected vegetable.

For a lighter version, substitute light cream, half-and-half, plain low-fat yogurt, buttermilk, or low-fat milk for the cream. Or omit any sort of dairy product and purée a cup of cooked white rice or potato along with the soup.

In a soup pot or large, heavy saucepan, melt the butter or heat the oil over medium heat. Add the onion or leek and sauté until golden and very soft, about 30 minutes. Add the asparagus or other vegetable and sauté for about 5 minutes. Add the stock or broth and bring to a boil over medium-high heat. Reduce the heat to low, cover partially, and simmer until the vegetable is very tender, about 25 to 45 minutes, depending on the type, size, and age of the vegetable. Remove from heat and cool slightly.

Working in batches, if necessary, transfer the soup to a food processor or blender and purée until smooth. Strain through a medium-mesh sieve into a clean pot, if serving the soup hot, or into a large bowl, if serving the soup cold; with a large spoon, press the vegetable pulp against the sides of the sieve to release as much liquid as possible. Stir in the cream and season to taste with salt and pepper.

To serve hot, heat over medium-low. Ladle into preheated soup bowls, garnish with asparagus or herb sprigs and flowers, if using, and serve immediately. Alternatively, pour into a container and refrigerate, uncovered, until cool, then tightly cover and store for up to 3 days. Slowly reheat before garnishing and serving.

To serve cold, pour into a container and refrigerate, uncovered, until cool, then tightly cover and chill for at least 2 hours or up to 3 days. Ladle into chilled bowls and garnish as for hot soup.

Serves 4 to 6 as a soup course, or 2 or 3 as a main dish.

Spring Pea Soup

About 12 tender lettuce leaves
6 cups Vegetable Stock (page 13),
   Poultry Stock (page 10), or
   3 cups canned chicken broth,
   preferably low-salt type, diluted
   with 3 cups water
2 cups chopped lettuce
1 cup chopped fresh mint or sorrel
Zest from 1 lemon
Salt
Freshly ground black pepper
2 cups fresh or thawed frozen
   shelled green peas
4 ounces snow peas, stemmed,
   stringed, and cut into julienne
Shredded fresh mint or young sorrel
   for garnish
Slivered prosciutto or baked ham
   for garnish (optional)

Soup that looks and tastes as delicate as a beautiful spring day!

Rinse the lettuce leaves in cold water and dry them well; wrap the leaves in a towel and chill them to crisp.

In a soup pot or large saucepan, combine the stock or broth, chopped lettuce, chopped mint or sorrel, and lemon zest. Bring to a boil over medium-high heat. Remove from heat and let stand for about 20 minutes. Strain into a pot and discard the greens and lemon zest. Season to taste with salt and pepper.

Bring the strained stock to a boil over medium-high heat. Reduce the heat to low, add the shelled peas and snow peas, and simmer until the peas are crisp-tender, about 2 minutes.

To serve hot, line individual bowls with lettuce leaves, ladle in the soup, and garnish with shredded mint and ham, if using. Alternatively, pour the strained stock into a container and refrigerate, uncovered, until cool, then cover tightly and store up to 3 days. Add peas and slowly reheat before garnishing and serving.

To serve cold, pour the soup into a container and refrigerate, uncovered, until cool, then tightly cover and chill for at least 2 hours or up to 3 days. Ladle into chilled lettuce-lined bowls and garnish as for hot soup.

Serves 6 as a soup course, or 3 or 4 as a main dish.

Potato-Sorrel Soup

Tart fresh sorrel is a welcome sign of spring.

In a soup pot or large, heavy saucepan, melt the butter over medium heat. Add the leek and sauté until soft but not browned, about 5 minutes. Add the potato slices and stock or broth. Bring to a boil, then cover, reduce the heat to low, and simmer until the potatoes are very soft, about 30 minutes.

In a small bowl, combine the crème fraîche or sour cream and tomato paste. Whisk in enough milk to make the mixture light and creamy. Set aside.

Working in batches, if necessary, transfer the soup to a food processor or blender, add the sorrel, and purée until very smooth. Pour into a clean pot, stir in the cream, and season to taste with salt and pepper.

To serve hot, heat over medium heat; do not allow the soup to come to a boil. Ladle into preheated bowls, add a dollop of the tomato cream to each serving, and swirl the cream into the soup with a wooden skewer or the tip of a sharp knife. Garnish with sorrel leaves. Alternatively, pour into a container and refrigerate, uncovered, until cool, then tightly cover and chill for at least 2 hours or up to 3 days. Slowly reheat before garnishing and serving.

To serve cold, pour into a container and refrigerate, uncovered, until cool, then tightly cover and chill for at least 2 hours or up to 3 days. Just before serving, whisk to blend well, then adjust seasonings, if necessary. Ladle into chilled bowls and garnish as for hot soup.

Serves 4 to 6 as a soup course, or 2 or 3 as a main course.

2 tablespoons unsalted butter
3 cups chopped leek, including
   pale green portion
   (about 2 large leeks)
1 pound white boiling or
   baking potatoes, peeled and
   thinly sliced
4 cups Vegetable Stock (page 13),
   Poultry Stock (page 10), or
   canned chicken broth,
   preferably low-salt type
¼ cup crème fraîche or sour cream
2 teaspoons tomato paste
About 1 tablespoon milk
4 cups coarsely chopped fresh sorrel
   (about 4 ounces)
½ cup heavy (whipping) cream,
   light cream, or half-and-half
Salt
Freshly ground white pepper
Small whole fresh sorrel leaves
   for garnish

Gingered Carrot Soup

During my days of running the Twin Peaks Gourmet in San Francisco, we made countless vats of this soup, which we sold freshly made or frozen. Although I prefer it as a refreshing cold dish on a summer day, it is also good hot.

To make the curly orange zest garnish shown, cut the peel from an orange with a citrus zester in a long continuous strip. Wind the zest around a drinking straw, wrap in plastic wrap, and refrigerate for about 30 minutes. Just before serving, unwrap and slide out the straw.

In a soup pot or large, heavy saucepan, melt the butter over medium-high heat. Add the leek and ginger and sauté until the leek is tender but not browned, about 5 minutes. Add the carrots and sauté until coated with butter. Stir in the stock or broth and bring to a boil. Reduce the heat to low, cover, and simmer until the carrots are very tender, about 30 minutes.

Working in batches, if necessary, transfer the soup to a food processor or blender and purée until smooth. Add the orange juice and blend well. Stir in the chopped mint and season to taste with salt and pepper.

To serve hot, pour the soup into a clean pot and heat over low heat. Garnish with citrus slices, mint sprigs, and orange zest. Alternatively, pour into a container and refrigerate, uncovered, until cool, then tightly cover and store as long as overnight. Slowly reheat before garnishing and serving.

To serve cold, pour into a container and refrigerate, uncovered, until cool, then tightly cover and chill for at least 2 hours or as long as overnight. Ladle into chilled bowls and garnish as for hot soup.

Serves 4 to 6 as a soup course, or 2 or 3 as a main course.

3 tablespoons unsalted butter
1 cup sliced leek, including pale green portion, or white onion
1 tablespoon minced peeled fresh ginger
1½ pounds (about 9) carrots, peeled, and cut into 1-inch lengths
2 cups Poultry Stock (page 10) or canned chicken broth, preferably low-salt type
2 cups freshly squeezed orange juice
¼ cup chopped fresh mint
Salt
Freshly ground white pepper
Fresh citrus slices such as blood oranges or kumquats for garnish
Fresh mint sprigs for garnish
Fresh orange zest, cut into julienne, for garnish

Cucumber-Yogurt Soup

4 cups peeled, seeded, and
    coarsely chopped cucumber
    (about 5 medium-sized or
    1 large English type)
½ cup coarsely chopped green onion
    (about 3), including green tops
2 tablespoons chopped fresh
    dill or mint
¼ cup freshly squeezed lemon juice
1 cup Vegetable Stock (page 13),
    Poultry Stock (page 10),
    Meat Stock (page 11), preferably
    made with lamb, or canned beef
    or chicken broth, preferably
    low-salt type
4 cups plain low-fat yogurt
Salt
Freshly ground white pepper
Fresh radish slices for garnish
Chopped fresh dill or mint
    for garnish

If you use the mildly flavored long English cucumbers, there's no need to peel or remove seeds.

Working in batches, if necessary, combine the cucumber, onion, dill or mint, lemon juice, and stock or broth in a food processor or blender and purée. Add the yogurt and blend until fairly smooth. Season to taste with salt and pepper.

To serve hot, pour the soup into a saucepan and heat over low heat; do not boil. Ladle into preheated bowls, garnish with radish and dill or mint, and serve immediately. Alternatively, pour from the food processor or blender into a container, tightly cover, and refrigerate for up to 3 days. Slowly reheat before garnishing and serving.

To serve cold, pour into a container, tightly cover, and chill for at least 2 hours or as long as 3 days. Ladle into chilled bowls and garnish as for hot soup.

Serves 6 as a soup course, or 3 or 4 as a main dish.

Red Pepper and Tomato Soup

If you enjoy a spicier soup, add chopped fresh red hot chile or dried chili flakes to taste along with the sweet pepper. For a golden soup, use golden sweet peppers and yellow tomato varieties.

Heat the olive oil in a soup pot or large, heavy saucepan over medium heat. Add the onion, chopped pepper, and garlic; stir to coat with the oil. Reduce the heat to low, cover, and cook, stirring occasionally, until the onion and pepper are soft and have just begun to color, about 30 minutes. Remove the cover, add the tomato, herbs, bay leaves, water, cumin, ginger, and salt and pepper to taste. Increase the heat to medium and bring to a boil, then lower the heat to low and simmer, uncovered, for about 45 minutes.

To make the pepper curl garnish, discard the stems, seeds, and membrane from the peppers. Slice the peppers lengthwise into very thin julienne. Place in a bowl of iced water and refrigerate for several hours to curl. Drain well before using.

Remove the soup from heat and cool slightly. Transfer the soup to a food processor or blender and purée until well blended.

To serve hot, pour the soup into a clean pot and simmer over medium heat. Ladle into warmed bowls and garnish each with a dollop of crème fraîche or sour cream. Alternatively, pour into a container and refrigerate, uncovered, until cool, then tightly cover and store for up to 3 days. Slowly reheat before garnishing and serving.

To serve cold, pour into a container and refrigerate, uncovered, until cool, then tightly cover and chill for at least 2 hours or up to 2 days. Ladle into chilled bowls and garnish each with several reserved pepper curls and a nasturtium or other flower.

Serves 4 to 6 as a soup course, or 2 or 3 as a main dish.

¼ cup olive oil,
 preferably extra-virgin
2 cups chopped red onion
4 cups chopped red sweet pepper
 (about 1⅓ pounds)
1 tablespoon chopped garlic
2 cups peeled, seeded, and chopped
 ripe tomato (about 1¼ pounds)
 or drained canned plum tomato
1 tablespoon minced mixed fresh
 herbs such as marjoram,
 rosemary, and thyme, or
 1 teaspoon crumbled mixed
 dried herbs such as
 herbes de Provence
2 bay leaves, crumbled
4 cups Vegetable Stock (page 13),
 Poultry Stock (page 10), or
 2 cups canned chicken broth
 diluted with 2 cups water
1 teaspoon ground cumin
1 tablespoon minced peeled
 fresh ginger
Salt
Freshly ground black pepper
½ *each* red and golden sweet pepper
 for garnish for cold soup
Crème fraîche or sour cream, if
 serving soup hot
Pesticide-free nasturtiums or other
 edible flowers for garnish,
 if serving soup cold (optional)

Fresh Herb and Garlic Soup with Croutons

1 French-style baguette, sliced about
   ½ inch thick and cut into cubes
Olive oil, preferably extra-virgin
2 quarts Vegetable Stock (page 13),
   Poultry Stock (page 10), or
   canned chicken broth,
   preferably low-salt type
40 garlic cloves, peeled and crushed
1 cup chopped fresh marjoram,
   savory, rosemary, thyme or
   other favorite herb, or a
   combination
½ cup heavy (whipping) cream
Salt
Freshly ground white pepper
2 cups freshly shredded Gruyère
   cheese (about 6 ounces)
Fresh herb sprigs for garnish (choose
   same herb or herbs used in soup)

This simple soup was suggested by similar versions from Spain and Portugal. Make it only when fresh herbs are available.

Preheat an oven to 350° F.

To make the croutons, brush the bread cubes all over with olive oil. Spread in a single layer on a baking sheet and bake until lightly golden, about 10 minutes. Set aside.

In a soup pot or large saucepan, combine the stock or broth, garlic, and herbs. Bring to a boil over medium-high heat, then adjust heat to maintain a gentle boil and cook until the garlic is very soft, about 20 minutes. Strain through a wire sieve into a saucepan, pressing the garlic and herbs to release all liquid; discard the garlic and herbs. Stir in the cream and heat over medium-low heat; do not boil. Season to taste with salt and pepper.

To serve, ladle the soup into preheated bowls, add several croutons, sprinkle with a portion of the cheese and herb sprigs, and serve immediately. Alternatively, pour into a container and refrigerate, uncovered, until cool, then tightly cover and store for up to 3 days. Slowly reheat before adding croutons, cheese, and garnish.

Serves 6 as a soup course, or 3 or 4 as a main dish.

Bread and Tomato Soup

1½ cups olive oil,
    preferably extra-virgin
1 tablespoon minced or pressed garlic,
    or to taste
¾ cup minced fresh rosemary or sage
10 ounces stale French or Italian
    bread, thinly sliced into about
    20 slices
4 cups chopped peeled and seeded
    fresh tomato (about 3 pounds)
    or drained canned plum tomato
2 quarts Meat Stock (page 11),
    preferably made with veal, or
    1 quart canned beef broth,
    preferably low-salt type, diluted
    with 1 quart water or dry white
    wine
Salt
Freshly ground black pepper
Fresh rosemary or sage sprigs
    for garnish
Freshly grated Parmesan cheese,
    preferably Parmigiano-
    Reggiano, for sprinkling over
    soup

European peasant soup originated as a bowl of stale bread covered with broth. This ancient recipe from the Tuscan region of Italy is a good example. Be sure to use good crusty bread, high-quality olive oil, and flavorful tomatoes.

This is a soup that should be eaten right after cooking, as the bread disintegrates when chilled and reheated.

In a large sauté pan or skillet, heat the oil over medium heat. Add the garlic and herb and sauté for about 1 minute; do not let the garlic brown. Add the bread and cook until golden brown on the bottom, then turn and cook until the other side is golden. Remove from heat and set aside.

In a soup pot or large, heavy saucepan, heat the tomato over high heat and cook for about 3 minutes. Stir in the stock or diluted broth and bring to a boil. Season to taste with salt and pepper. Reduce the heat to low, stir in the bread, cover, and simmer for about 45 minutes.

Ladle into preheated bowls, garnish with herb sprigs, and serve immediately. Pass the cheese at the table.

Serves 8 as a soup course, or 4 or 5 as a main dish.

Broccoli- or Cauliflower-Cheese Soup

This recipe is based on an extremely rich soup served by my Aunt Doris in Jackson, Mississippi. I've modified the original recipe, which called for processed cheese and canned mushroom soup.

Place the broccoli or cauliflower in a steamer rack set over simmering water, cover, and steam until just tender, about 6 minutes. Remove from heat, rinse with cold water to stop the cooking and preserve color, and drain. Chop finely and set aside.

In a soup pot or large, heavy saucepan, melt 3 tablespoons of the butter over low heat. Add the flour and cook, stirring constantly, for about 3 minutes. Whisk in the stock or broth and cream or half-and-half. Increase the heat to medium-high and bring to a boil, stirring or whisking constantly. Reduce the heat to low and simmer, stirring occasionally, until thickened, about 10 minutes. Season to taste with salt and pepper.

Meanwhile, in a sauté pan or skillet, heat the remaining 3 tablespoons butter over low heat. Add the onion and sauté until soft but not golden, about 8 minutes. Add the garlic, mushrooms, and chile and sauté until the mushrooms are soft, about 5 minutes longer. Transfer to the cream mixture. Add the broccoli or cauliflower and the cheeses and cook over low heat, stirring almost constantly, until cheese melts, about 5 minutes; do not allow to approach a boil. Season to taste with salt and pepper.

Ladle into preheated bowls, garnish with the ham, and serve hot. Alternatively, pour into a container and refrigerate, uncovered, until cool, then tightly cover and store up to 3 days. Slowly reheat, stirring frequently to keep cheese from curdling, before garnishing and serving.

Serves 6 to 8 as a soup course, or 3 or 4 as a main dish.

1 pound broccoli or cauliflower, coarsely chopped
6 tablespoons (¾ stick) unsalted butter
¼ cup all-purpose flour
4 cups Poultry Stock (page 10) or canned chicken broth, preferably low-salt type
2 cups heavy (whipping) cream, light cream, or half-and-half
Salt
Freshly ground black pepper
1 cup chopped yellow onion
1 tablespoon minced or pressed garlic
½ pound fresh mushrooms, chopped
3 tablespoons minced fresh or canned jalapeño chiles, or to taste
1 cup freshly shredded cheddar cheese (about 3 ounces)
1 cup freshly shredded Emmentaler or Jarlsberg cheese (about 3 ounces)
Slivered baked ham for garnish

Japanese Eggplant-Miso Soup

Instant fish soup stock (*dashi-no-moto*) and other Japanese ingredients may be purchased from Asian groceries. Flavorful soybean paste or miso comes in white *(shiro miso),* yellow *(shinshu-miso),* red *(aka miso),* or brown *(hatcho miso);* flavors range from slightly sweet to slightly bitter. **Each makes good soup.**

In a soup pot or large, heavy saucepan, heat the oil over medium-high heat. Add the eggplant and mushrooms and sauté for 5 minutes. Add the stock or diluted broth and bring to a boil, then reduce the heat to low, cover, and simmer until the vegetables are very soft, about 20 minutes. Remove from heat and cool slightly. Transfer the mixture to a food processor or blender and purée. Add the soybean paste and blend until smooth. Pour the soup into a clean pot. Thin with additional stock or water if too thick. Season to taste with salt. Heat over medium-low heat.

Ladle the soup into preheated bowls, garnish with the mushrooms and *shiso,* if using, and serve immediately. Alternatively, pour into a container and refrigerate, uncovered, until cool, then tightly cover and store up to 3 days. Slowly reheat before garnishing and serving.

Serves 6 as a soup course, or 3 or 4 as a main dish.

3 tablespoons high-quality vegetable oil such as safflower
3 cups peeled and sliced eggplant, preferably slender Asian-type (about 1 pound)
½ pound fresh enoki or shiitake mushrooms
4 cups reconstituted Japanese soup stock *(dashi-no-moto),* Poultry Stock (page 10), or 2 cups canned chicken broth, preferably low-salt type, diluted with 2 cups water
¼ cup fermented soybean paste (miso)
Salt
Enoki mushrooms for garnish
Fresh *shiso* (minty Japanese herb) leaves for garnish (optional)

Wild Mushroom Soup

Thanks to the efforts of mushroom growers and distributors, we no longer have to forage the wilds for flavorful mushroom varieties. If only common white mushrooms are available, however, combine 1½ pounds fresh with ½ pound dried wild mushrooms that have been reconstituted by soaking in warm water until soft; rinse well to remove grit and discard tough stems.

Discard the tough ends from the mushroom stems. Clean the mushrooms with moist paper toweling. Coarsely chop or thinly slice the mushrooms.

In a soup pot or large, heavy saucepan, melt the butter over medium heat. Add the mushrooms and sauté until they are soft and have released their moisture, about 5 minutes. Stir in the flour and cook, stirring, for about 1 minute longer.

Add the stock or broth and bring the soup to a boil over high heat. Reduce the heat to low, stir in the marjoram or thyme, and season to taste with salt, pepper, and nutmeg. Cover and simmer, stirring occasionally, until the mushrooms are tender, about 20 minutes.

Stir in the sherry and ladle into preheated bowls, garnish with the herb, and serve immediately. Alternatively, pour into a container and refrigerate, uncovered, until cool, then tightly cover and store as long as 3 days. Slowly reheat before garnishing and serving.

To serve the soup under a puff pastry dome, cook the soup only about 10 minutes after adding the stock and seasonings to the mushrooms; stir in the sherry, ladle into ovenproof bowls, and chill. Preheat an oven to 400° F. Cut rounds of puff pastry slightly larger than the diameter of the bowls. Cover the bowls and bring the edges down over the sides and press to adhere to the bowl. Brush the pastry with beaten egg and bake until golden brown and crisp, about 40 minutes. Serve immediately.

Serves 6 as a soup course, or 3 or 4 as a main dish.

2 pounds fresh mushrooms such as chanterelles, morels, porcini, or shiitakes
3 tablespoons unsalted butter
2 tablespoons all-purpose flour
2 quarts Meat Stock (page 11) or canned beef broth, preferably low-salt type
2 tablespoons minced fresh marjoram or thyme, or 2 teaspoons dried marjoram or thyme
Salt
Freshly ground black pepper
Freshly grated nutmeg
3 tablespoons dry sherry, or to taste
Minced fresh marjoram or thyme for garnish
1 pound freshly made or thawed frozen puff pastry (optional)
1 egg, beaten, for glaze (optional)

Creamy Cabbage Soup

½ cup (1 stick) unsalted butter
1 large cabbage, cored and shredded
2 quarts milk
Salt
Freshly ground black pepper
½ pound smoked hot pork sausage,
    sliced (optional)
¼ cup water (optional)

My partner, Lin Cotton, introduced me to cabbage simmered in milk and butter. I've turned that simple but rich dish into a satisfying porridge.

Instead of adding the sausage to the soup, you might wish to sprinkle crumbled crisply cooked bacon over each serving.

In a soup pot or large, heavy saucepan, melt the butter over medium-high heat. Add the cabbage and sauté for about 2 minutes. Stir in the milk and salt and pepper to taste; be generous with the pepper. Reduce the heat to low, cover, and simmer until the cabbage is very tender and the soup is creamy, about 1 hour.

Meanwhile, combine the sausage and water in a sauté pan or skillet. Cook over medium-high heat until the water evaporates. Reduce the heat to low and continue cooking until the sausage renders its fat and is lightly browned, about 5 minutes. Transfer with a slotted utensil to paper toweling to drain. Add to the soup about 15 minutes before it is ready to serve.

Ladle the soup into preheated bowls and serve immediately. Alternatively, pour into a container and refrigerate, uncovered, until cool, then tightly cover and store for up to 2 days. Slowly reheat before serving.

Serves 6 as a soup course, or 3 or 4 as a main dish.

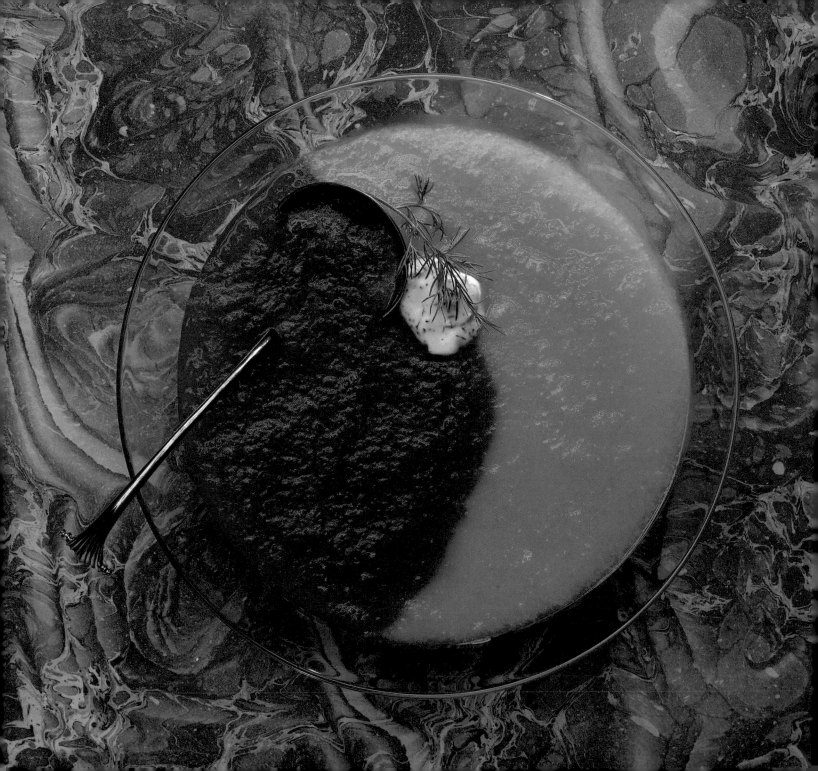

Creamy Beet Borscht

Puréed vegetables account for the creaminess of this soup. For a two-toned presentation, prepare a batch of borscht with red beets and red tomatoes and make another batch using golden beets, golden tomatoes, and white instead of red vinegar. Ladle the two soups simultaneously into each bowl.

In a soup pot or large, heavy saucepan, heat the oil or melt the butter over medium-high heat. Add the onion and sauté until soft but not browned, about 5 minutes. Add the garlic, sugar, and vinegar and cook until the vinegar evaporates, about 3 minutes. Add the beets, tomato, potato, carrot or parsnip, 5 cups stock or broth, and salt and pepper to taste. Bring to a boil, then reduce the heat to low, cover, and simmer until the vegetables are very tender, about 30 to 40 minutes. Remove from heat and cool slightly.

Combine the minced herb and cream in a small bowl; set aside.

Working in batches, if necessary, transfer the soup to a food processor or blender and purée until smooth. Thin with additional stock or broth if the mixture is too thick.

To serve hot, transfer the purée to a clean pot and heat over low heat. Ladle into preheated bowls, drizzle each serving with a portion of the herbed cream, and draw a wooden skewer or the tip of a sharp knife through the cream to create a pattern. Garnish with herb sprigs and serve immediately. Alternatively, pour into a container and refrigerate, uncovered, until cool, then tightly cover and store for up to 3 days. Slowly reheat before garnishing and serving.

To serve cold, pour into a container and refrigerate, uncovered, until cool, then tightly cover and chill for at least 2 hours or up to 3 days. Ladle into chilled bowls and garnish as for hot soup.

Serves 6 to 8 as a soup course, or 3 or 4 as a main dish.

2 tablespoons olive oil or unsalted butter
1 cup chopped onion
1 teaspoon minced or pressed garlic
1 teaspoon sugar
3 tablespoons balsamic or red wine vinegar
1½ pounds beets (about 6 medium-sized), peeled and shredded or coarsely chopped
2 cups chopped peeled and seeded fresh tomato (about 1¼ pounds) or drained canned tomato
1 cup coarsely chopped peeled potato (about 1 medium-sized)
½ cup coarsely chopped peeled carrot or parsnip (about 1 small)
About 5 cups Meat Stock (page 11), made with beef, Poultry Stock (page 10), or canned beef or chicken broth, preferably low-salt type
Salt
Freshly ground black pepper
¼ cup minced fresh dill or basil
⅓ cup crème fraîche, sour cream, or whipped heavy cream
Fresh dill or herb sprigs for garnish

Underground Soup

3 tablespoons olive oil
1½ cups chopped onion
1 teaspoon minced or pressed garlic
6 cups Vegetable Stock (page 13),
　　Poultry Stock (page 10), or
　　canned chicken broth,
　　preferably low-salt type
1 cup diced turnip or rutabaga
1 cup diced peeled sweet potato
1 cup diced peeled carrot
Salt
Freshly ground black pepper
1 cup diced peeled celery root
2 chicken breast halves, skinned,
　　boned, and cut into bite-sized
　　pieces (optional)
3 tablespoons chopped fresh tarragon
　　or fennel greens
Fresh tarragon or fennel sprigs
　　for garnish

The vegetables in this hearty soup all grow underground. Although good with only vegetables, the soup is even better with poached chicken breast.

In a soup pot or large, heavy saucepan, heat the oil over low heat. Add the onion, cover, and cook, stirring occasionally, until the onion is soft and just beginning to color, about 30 minutes. Remove the cover, increase the heat to medium, add the garlic, and sauté until the onion is golden, about 20 minutes.

Stir in the stock or broth, turnip or rutabaga, sweet potato, and carrot and bring to a boil. Reduce the heat to low, cover partially, and simmer until the vegetables are crisp-tender, about 20 minutes. Season to taste with salt and pepper.

Add the celery root and chicken, if using, and continue to simmer until all the vegetables are tender but still hold their shape and the chicken is opaque, about 10 minutes. About 5 minutes before the soup is done, stir in the tarragon or fennel.

Ladle into preheated bowls, garnish with tarragon or fennel sprigs, and serve immediately. Alternatively, pour into a container and refrigerate, uncovered, until cool, then tightly cover and store for up to 3 days. Slowly reheat before garnishing and serving.

Serves 6 as a soup course, or 3 or 4 as a main dish.

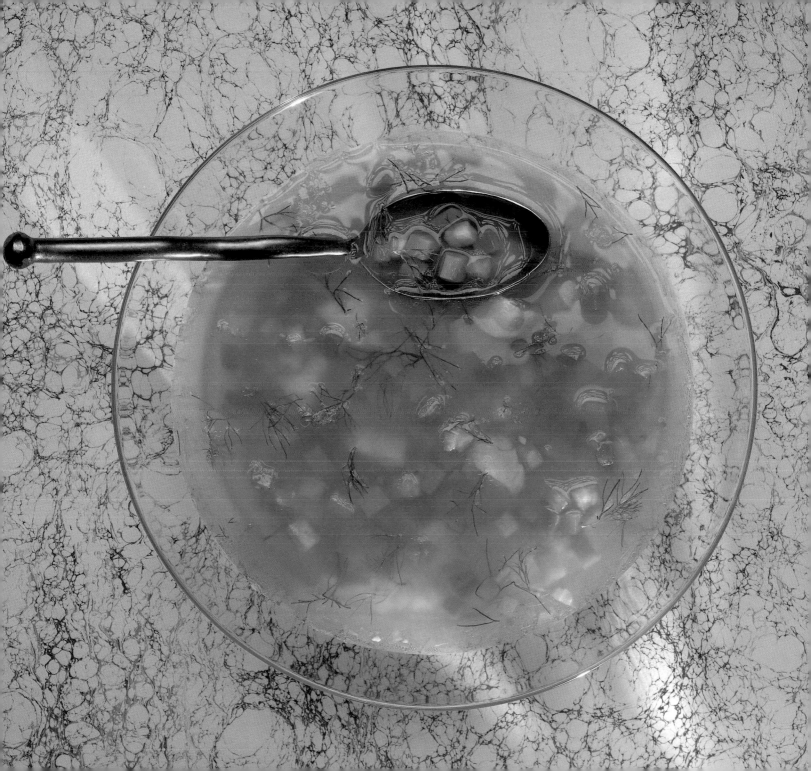

Onion and Cider Soup Gratin

½ cup (1 stick) unsalted butter
5 cups thinly sliced yellow onion
4 cups hard cider
4 cups Meat Stock (page 11),
    Poultry Stock (page 10), or
    canned beef or chicken broth,
    preferably low-salt type
Salt
Freshly ground black pepper
1 French baguette, sliced about
    ½ inch thick
2½ cups freshly shredded firm,
    smooth cheese such as cheddar,
    Cantal, Emmentaler, or Gouda
    (about 8 ounces), or crumbled
    blue cheese such as Stilton

One of the best versions of this classic that I've eaten was at Metropolis in Toronto, where the cider imparted an aromatic flavor complemented by a mixture of the finest cheddar blended with two cheeses from Canadian monasteries: Oka and St. Benoit. Use a combination of favorite melting cheeses; blue-veined is great.

The toasted bread rounds can be prepared up to 2 days ahead and stored in an airtight container.

In a soup pot or large, heavy saucepan, melt ¼ cup (4 tablespoons) of the butter over low heat. Add the onion, cover, and cook, stirring occasionally, until soft and just beginning to color, about 25 minutes. Uncover and increase heat to medium and cook until onion is deep golden and almost caramelized, about 25 minutes longer.

Add the cider and stock to the caramelized onion and bring to a boil over medium-high heat. Season to taste with salt and pepper. Reduce the heat to low and simmer, uncovered, for 30 minutes. (At this point, the soup can be refrigerated, uncovered, until cool, then tightly covered and stored for up to 3 days; reheat before proceeding.)

Preheat an oven to 325° F.

Melt the remaining ¼ cup of the butter and brush both sides of the bread slices. Arrange the bread in a single layer on a baking sheet and bake until crisp and golden, about 25 minutes.

Just before serving, heat the soup to boiling. Preheat a broiler.

Place 3 slices of toasted bread in the bottom of each individual heat-resistant bowl or crock. Ladle the soup into the bowls, sprinkle a portion of cheese on top of each serving, and place under the broiler until the cheese is bubbly and beginning to brown, 2 to 3 minutes. Serve piping hot.

Serves 6 to 8 as a soup course, or 3 or 4 as a main dish.

Creamy Bean Soup

2 cups dried beans
¼ cup olive oil
1 cup chopped yellow onion
1 tablespoon chopped fresh or canned
 jalapeño or other hot chile, or
 to taste
2 teaspoons minced or pressed garlic
1 tablespoon minced fresh oregano,
 or 1 teaspoon crumbled dried
 oregano
1 tablespoon minced fresh thyme, or
 1 teaspoon crumbled dried
 thyme
1½ teaspoons ground cumin
1 teaspoon ground coriander
3 bay leaves
3 quarts Poultry Stock (page 10),
 Vegetable Stock (page 13),
 water, or 6 cups canned chicken
 broth, preferably low-salt type,
 diluted with 6 cups water
½ cup tomato purée (optional)
Salt
Freshly ground black pepper

Any dried beans can be used for this soup. For the photograph, I combined two versions of the recipe: one made with black beans and another made with white beans. After pouring them simultaneously into the bowl, I quickly swirled a wooden skewer through the soups to create a pattern, then drizzled on puréed roasted red pepper and swirled it through.

When making soup with white beans, you may choose to omit the tomato purée if you desire a whiter soup. For an even whiter and creamier version, drain the beans before puréeing and blend with light or heavy (whipping) cream to create the desired consistency. For a chunky soup, serve when the beans are tender; do not purée.

Carefully pick over the beans to remove any shriveled beans and foreign matter. Rinse, cover with cold water, and soak overnght. Drain and set aside.

In a soup pot or large, heavy saucepan, heat the oil over medium-high heat. Add the onion and chile and sauté until soft, about 5 minutes. Add the garlic, oregano, thyme, cumin, and coriander and sauté 1 minute longer. Add the beans, bay leaves, and stock, water, or diluted broth. Bring to a boil, then reduce heat, cover, and simmer for 1½ hours.

Stir the tomato purée into the beans and season to taste with salt and pepper. Cover and simmer until the beans begin to fall apart, about 1½ hours longer; add more liquid if necessary to keep beans covered during cooking.

Working in batches, if necessary, transfer the beans and their liquid to a food processor or blender and purée, adding extra stock, water, or diluted broth as needed to make a fairly smooth purée. Pour into a clean pot and heat over low heat. Serve hot. Alternatively, pour into a container and refrigerate, uncovered, until cool, then tightly cover and store for up to 3 days. Slowly reheat before serving.

Serves 4 to 6 as a soup course, or 2 or 3 as a main dish.

Pasta and Bean Soup

Italian *pasta e fagioli* is a hearty combination of pasta and beans. To vary the soup, substitute other dried beans and pasta shapes.

Carefully pick over the beans to remove any shriveled beans and foreign matter. Rinse, cover with cold water, and soak overnight. Drain and set aside.

In a soup pot or large, heavy saucepan, heat 2 tablespoons of the oil over medium-high heat. Add the onion and celery and sauté until soft, about 5 minutes. Add the garlic, sage, and rosemary and sauté 1 minute longer. Add the bay leaves, drained beans, and enough water to cover by about 1 inch. Bring to a boil, then reduce heat, cover, and simmer 1½ hours.

In a sauté pan or skillet, heat the remaining 3 tablespoons olive oil over medium-high heat. Add the *pancetta* or ham, carrot, and fennel, if using, and sauté until the *pancetta* is cooked, about 5 minutes. Add the mixture to the beans. Stir in the tomato, parsley, and stock or broth and season to taste with salt and pepper. Cover and simmer until the beans are very tender, about 1 hour longer; add more liquid if necessary to keep the beans covered during cooking.

About 20 minutes before the soup is ready to serve, increase the heat and bring the soup to a boil. Stir in the macaroni and cook until *al dente*. Just before serving, stir in the minced basil or fennel greens.

Ladle the soup into preheated bowls, sprinkle with Parmesan cheese, and garnish with basil or fennel sprigs. Pass additional cheese at the table. Alternatively, pour the soup into a container and refrigerate, uncovered, until cool, then tightly cover and store for up to 3 days. Slowly reheat before adding herbs, cheese, and garnish.

Serves 4 to 6 as a soup course, or 2 or 3 as a main dish.

1 cup dried white *cannellini* beans
5 tablespoons olive oil
1 cup finely chopped yellow onion
½ cup finely chopped celery
1 teaspoon minced or pressed garlic
¼ cup minced fresh sage, or
    1 tablespoon crumbled dried
    sage
1 tablespoon minced fresh rosemary,
    or 1 teaspoon crumbled dried
    rosemary
2 bay leaves
3 ounces *pancetta* (Italian bacon)
    or baked ham, chopped
    (about 1 cup)
1 cup diced peeled carrot
½ cup chopped fennel bulb (optional)
½ cup chopped fresh or drained
    canned plum tomato
3 tablespoons minced fresh parsley,
    preferably flat-leaf type
2 cups Meat Stock (page 11),
    Poultry Stock (page 10), or
    canned beef or chicken broth,
    preferably low-salt type
Salt
Freshly ground black pepper
¾ cup any small dried macaroni
3 tablespoons minced fresh basil or
    fennel greens
Freshly grated Parmesan cheese,
    preferably Parmigiano-
    Reggiano
Fresh basil or fennel sprigs for
    garnish

Fish, Poultry, & Meat Soups

Spicy Seafood Soup

1 pound raw medium-sized shrimp
1 tablespoon safflower or other
    high-quality vegetable oil
2 quarts Fish Stock (page 12),
    Poultry Stock (page 10), or
    1 quart canned chicken broth,
    preferably low-salt type,
    combined with 1 quart water
3 fresh lemon grass stalks, coarsely
    chopped, or 3 tablespoons
    grated lemon zest
Grated zest from 1 lime
6 to 8 kaffir lime leaves or fresh lemon
    or lime leaves
10 slices unpeeled fresh, thawed
    frozen, or dried *galangal (kah*
    or laos) or fresh ginger root,
    sliced about ⅛ inch thick
2 fresh Serrano or other hot chiles,
    stemmed, seeded, and chopped
24 small to medium-sized mussels or
    clams in shells, scrubbed
    (mussels debearded)
2 tablespoons freshly squeezed
    lime juice
2 tablespoons fish sauce, or
    1 tablespoon light soy sauce
3 tablespoons chopped fresh cilantro
    (coriander)
1 tablespoon slivered fresh red hot
    chile, or to taste
¼ cup chopped green onion
Salt
Thin lime slices for garnish
Fresh lime or other citrus leaves and
    blossoms for garnish

Inspiration for this highly fragrant soup came from several versions of similar soups enjoyed in Thai restaurants. Thai ingredients are available wherever foods from Southeast Asia are sold; I've suggested some substitutes that will render a similar, albeit less flavorful, finished soup. Cracked crab or lobster, sliced squid, or oysters may be added and cooked in the simmering broth.

Peel and devein the shrimp; cover and refrigerate the shrimp and reserve the shells.

Heat the oil in a soup pot or large, heavy saucepan over high heat. Add the shrimp shells and sauté until the shells turn bright pink. Add the stock or diluted broth, lemon grass or zest, lime zest and leaves, *galangal* or ginger, and chiles or chile. Bring to a boil, then reduce heat to low, cover, and simmer for 25 minutes. Strain the broth through a fine sieve into a clean soup pot. (At this point, the soup can be poured into a container and refrigerated, uncovered, until cool, then tightly covered and stored for up to 3 days. Slowly reheat before proceeding.)

Bring the strained soup to a boil over high heat. Add the mussels or clams, cover, and cook until the shells open, about 2 minutes. Remove the mussels or clams and break off and discard the top shell. Return the mussels or clams on the half shell to the broth. Add the shrimp and cook until the shrimp turn opaque, about 2 minutes. Reduce the heat to low, stir in the lime juice, fish sauce, cilantro, slivered chile, green onion, and salt to taste; simmer about 1 minute. Ladle into preheated soup bowls, garnish with lime slices, leaves, and blossoms, and serve immediately.

Serves 6 as a soup course, or 3 or 4 as a main dish.

Saffron Scallop Soup

This creamy essence of the sea is enlivened by the special flavor and color of saffron.

In a soup pot or large, heavy saucepan, melt the butter over medium-high heat. Add the shallot and leek or onion and sauté until soft but not browned, about 5 minutes. Add the stock or diluted broth and saffron threads. Bring to a boil, then reduce the heat to low, cover, and simmer for about 15 minutes. Add the scallops and simmer until the scallops turn opaque, about 5 minutes. Remove from the heat and strain into a clean saucepan through a collander lined with several layers of dampened cheesecloth. Squeeze the cheesecloth to extract all the liquid. Set over medium heat.

In a bowl, combine the eggs and cream or half-and-half. Whisk in about ½ cup of the hot soup, then whisk the mixture into the hot soup. Season to taste with salt and pepper and cook, stirring quite frequently, until slightly thickened, about 15 to 20 minutes; do not allow to boil. Ladle into preheated bowls, garnish with lemon and leek, and serve immediately. Alternatively, pour the soup into a container and refrigerate, uncovered, until cool, then tightly cover and store up to overnight. Slowly reheat before serving; do not boil.

Serves 6 as a soup course, or 3 or 4 as a main dish.

3 tablespoons unsalted butter
3 tablespoons chopped shallot
1 cup sliced leek (white portion only)
    or white onion
4 cups Fish Stock (page 12) or 2 cups
    canned chicken broth,
    preferably low-salt type, diluted
    with 2 cups water or white wine
1 teaspoon saffron threads, or
    ½ teaspoon ground saffron, or
    to taste
2 pounds fresh scallops, chopped
2 egg yolks, beaten
1 cup heavy (whipping) or
    light cream or half-and-half
Salt
Freshly ground white pepper
Thin lemon slices for garnish
Julienned leek greens for garnish

Oyster and Artichoke Soup

4 large artichokes
¾ cup (1½ sticks) unsalted butter
⅔ cup chopped shallot, leek
    (including pale green portion)
    or yellow onion
1 cup sliced celery
4 cups Fish Stock (page 12),
    Poultry Stock (page 10), or
    2 cups canned chicken broth,
    preferably low-salt type, diluted
    with 2 cups water or dry white
    wine
¼ cup all-purpose flour
1 cup heavy (whipping) cream
Salt
Freshly ground black pepper
Ground cayenne pepper
About ¼ cup dry sherry
1 pint freshly shucked small to
    medium-sized oysters
Chopped fresh chives for garnish
Freshly grated Parmesan cheese for
    sprinkling (optional)

Ever since my roommate, Cary Griffin, and I used to play hooky from theological seminary chapel services in order to dine in one of New Orleans's fancy Creole restaurants, oysters and artichokes have been a favorite flavor combination of mine. This very rich soup should be served in small portions.

Boil, steam, or microwave the artichokes until tender. Pull off the leaves and scrape the pulp into a bowl. Discard the fuzzy choke and chop the bottoms. Set aside.

In a soup pot or large, heavy saucepan, melt ½ cup (1 stick) of the butter over medium heat. Add the shallot, leek, or onion and celery and sauté until soft but not golden, about 5 minutes. Add the artichoke pulp and sauté 1 minute longer. Stir in the stock or diluted broth and bring to a boil over medium-high heat, then reduce the heat to low and simmer for 15 minutes. Remove from the heat and cool slightly. Working in batches, if necessary, transfer the soup to a food processor or blender and purée until smooth. Pour the mixture into a clean pot and bring to a simmer over low heat.

In a small saucepan, melt the remaining ¼ cup butter over medium heat. Add the flour and cook, stirring constantly, until the mixture is smooth and lightly golden. Stir the mixture into the simmering soup and blend well. Stir in the cream and season to taste with salt, peppers, and sherry. Add the oysters and simmer until the oysters are cooked, about 4 minutes.

Ladle the soup into preheated bowls, garnish with chives, and serve immediately. Offer the cheese at the table, if desired. Alternatively, before adding the oysters, ladle the soup into a container and refrigerate, uncovered, until cool, then tightly cover and store for up to 3 days. Slowly reheat before adding oysters, garnishing, and serving.

Serves 8 as a soup course, or 4 to 6 as a main dish.

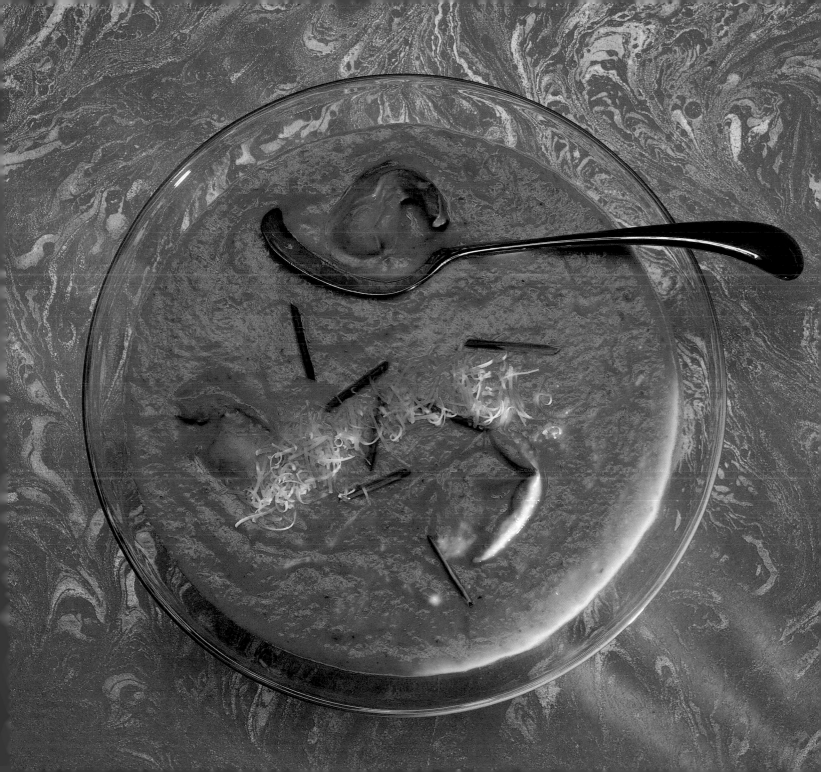

Caribbean Crab Callaloo

Countless variations and spellings of this soup are found throughout the islands of the Caribbean. There it is made with leaves of fresh callaloo, the common name for the leaves of dasheen or taro and other relatives of the calla lily. Other greens make acceptable substitutes. Check Asian markets for dasheen or taro or Chinese spinach, or use young Swiss chard or regular spinach.

Coconut milk may be substituted for a portion of the stock or broth.

If you wish to add traditional cornmeal dumplings, see the recipe on page 72 in my *Corn Cookbook,* or use another recipe. Spoon the batter into the soup along with the crab, cover the pot, and simmer until the dumplings are done.

In a soup pot or large, heavy saucepan, cook the bacon over medium heat until crisp. Transfer the bacon pieces to paper toweling to drain. Heat the drippings in the pot over low heat. Add the onions and cook until soft but not browned, about 10 minutes. Stir in the garlic, thyme, and okra and cook about 5 minutes longer.

Add the stock or broth and greens and bring to a boil over medium-high heat. Reduce the heat to low, cover, and simmer until the okra is almost tender, about 5 minutes. Stir in the crab meat and season to taste with salt, pepper, and pepper sauce; be generous with the pepper sauce. Continue to simmer until the crab is heated through and the greens are just tender but still retain their color. Ladle into preheated bowls, sprinkle with the reserved bacon, and serve immediately.

Alternatively, before adding the crab meat and greens, pour the soup into a container and refrigerate, uncovered, until cool, then cover tightly and store for up to 3 days. Slowly reheat, add the crab and greens, and continue as above.

Serves 6 as a soup course, or 3 or 4 as a main dish.

½ pound sliced bacon, chopped
1 cup finely chopped yellow onion
¼ cup finely chopped green onion, including green tops
½ teaspoon minced or pressed garlic
1 tablespoon minced fresh thyme, or 1 teaspoon crumbled dried thyme
½ pound fresh okra pods, stemmed and sliced about ½-inch thick, or 1 package (10 ounces) thawed frozen sliced okra
6 cups Fish Stock (page 12), Poultry Stock (page 10) or canned chicken broth, preferably low-salt type
1 pound fresh young spinach or other greens (see recipe introduction), thinly shredded
½ pound flaked cooked crab meat
Salt
Freshly ground black pepper
Tabasco or other red hot pepper sauce

Cambodian Red Chicken Soup with Pineapple

My initial taste of a similar preparation served at the Angkor Wat restaurant in San Francisco was love at first slurp.

Look for any unfamiliar ingredients in stores that specialize in foods from Southeast Asia. Tamarind may also be located in shops that sell foods imported from India, or in Hispanic markets, where it is labeled *tamarindo.*

To make the curry paste, soak the chile in warm water until soft, about 20 minutes. Drain, then combine with the remaining paste ingredients in a food processor or blender and blend into a thick paste. Transfer to a container, cover, and refrigerate until needed; the paste will keep for about 2 weeks (there will be enough for 2 batches of soup).

If using whole tamarind pods, peel the pods and place in a bowl. Strain and reserve the liquid. If using pulp, pinch off enough pulp to form a ball about 2 inches in diameter. Cover the pods or pulp with ½ cup hot water and let stand for 20 minutes; strain and reserve the liquid from the pods. If using pulp, knead it in water with your fingertips, then strain, pressing the pulp against the sides of a wire sieve with a large spoon to release all liquid. If using liquid concentrate, combine 1 tablespoon concentrate with 7 tablespoons water.

To make the soup, combine the stock or broth and coconut milk in a soup pot or large saucepan. Bring to a boil over medium-high heat, then reduce the heat to low. Stir 2 tablespoons of the curry paste into the simmering liquid until well blended. Add the tamarind liquid, pineapple, fish sauce, fresh and ground chile, and sugar. Simmer for about 4 minutes. Add the chicken and continue to simmer until the chicken is opaque; do not overcook the chicken. Stir in the mint just before serving.

Ladle the soup into preheated bowls and serve immediately. Alternatively, pour into a container and refrigerate, uncovered, until cool, then tightly cover and store for up to 3 days. Slowly reheat before serving.

Serves 6 as a soup course, or 3 or 4 as a main dish.

RED CURRY PASTE
1 large dried hot chile
1 fresh lemon grass stalk, coarsely chopped, or zest from 1 lemon
4 strips dried kaffir lime peel, or zest from 1 lime
10 peeled garlic cloves
2 slices unpeeled fresh, thawed frozen, or dried *galangal (kah* or *laos)* or fresh ginger root, sliced about ⅛ inch thick
½ teaspoon salt, or to taste
½ teaspoon dried shrimp paste
½ teaspoon ground coriander seeds
¼ teaspoon ground cumin

5 or 6 fresh ripe tamarind pods, about 3 tablespoons preserved tamarind pulp, or 1 tablespoon tamarind concentrate
2 cups Poultry Stock (page 10), made with chicken, or canned chicken broth, preferably low-salt type
2 cups canned unsweetened coconut milk
1½ cups coarsely chopped fresh pineapple
2 teaspoons fish sauce
1 fresh red hot chile, stems, seeds, and membrane discarded, chopped
1 teaspoon ground dried hot chile
2 teaspoons sugar
2 skinned and boned chicken breast halves, cut into bite-sized pieces
About ½ cup small fresh mint leaves or shredded fresh mint

Asian Chicken Noodle Soup

2 tablespoons peanut or other
high-quality vegetable oil
½ cup chopped yellow onion
2 tablespoons coarsely chopped
unpeeled fresh ginger
3 garlic cloves, smashed
1 cup coarsely chopped fresh cilantro
(coriander)
4 cups Poultry Stock,
Asian Variation (page 10),
or 2 cups canned chicken broth,
preferably low-salt type, diluted
with 2 cups water
2 or 3 star anise
About 3 cups water
1 small carrot, peeled and
cut into 2½-inch julienne
3 ounces fresh snow peas,
strings discarded, cut into
2½-inch julienne
1 medium-sized red sweet pepper,
stemmed, seeded, and cut into
2½-inch julienne
4 skinned and boned chicken breast
halves, sliced lengthwise into
long thin strips
4 ounces cellophane noodles
(mung bean threads), covered
with boiling water, soaked
5 minutes, and drained
About 2 tablespoons fish sauce, or
1 tablespoon light soy sauce
Toasted sesame seeds or dry-roasted
peanuts, coarsely chopped for
sprinkling
Whole star anise for garnish
Fresh cilantro sprigs for garnish
Lime or lemon wedges

Cooked rice, thin rice noodles, or any thin pasta may be substituted for the cellophane noodles, which are available from Asian markets. One pound thinly sliced beef may be substituted for the chicken; use stock made from beef.

In a wok or large, heavy saucepan, heat the oil over high heat. Add the onion and sauté until soft but not browned, about 4 minutes. Add the ginger, garlic, and cilantro and sauté about 1 minute longer. Stir in the stock or broth and star anise. Bring to a boil, then reduce the heat to low, cover, and simmer for about 20 minutes.

In a saucepan, bring the water to a boil over high heat. Add the vegetables, one type at a time, and blanch until crisp-tender. Remove the vegetables with a slotted utensil and plunge into ice water to stop cooking and preserve color. Reserve; drain before using.

Strain the soup into a clean pot, add the chicken, and bring to a boil over medium-high heat. Immediately reduce heat so the water barely ripples. Simmer until the chicken is opaque throughout, about 10 minutes. Add the drained noodles and simmer for about 2 minutes. Season to taste with fish sauce or soy sauce.

Ladle the noodles and soup into preheated bowls. Arrange 3 pieces of chicken in each bowl in a spoke pattern. Add the drained vegetables, placing them separately between each piece of chicken. Sprinkle with sesame seeds or peanuts, garnish with star anise and cilantro, and serve immediately. Offer lime or lemon to squeeze over soup.

Alternatively, do not soak the noodles or prepare the vegetables until shortly before serving. Pour the soup into a container and refrigerate, uncovered, until cool, then tightly cover and store up to 3 days. Slowly reheat while soaking noodles and blanching vegetables.

Serves 6 as a soup course, or 3 or 4 as a main dish.

Duck and Sausage Gumbo

⅔ cup all-purpose flour
⅔ cup safflower or other high-quality
    vegetable oil
1 cup chopped yellow onion
½ cup chopped green onion,
    including green tops
1 cup chopped celery
1 cup chopped green sweet pepper
1 pound fresh okra, sliced ¼ inch
    thick (optional)
1 tablespoon minced or pressed garlic
2 quarts Poultry Stock (page 10),
    preferably made with duck, or
    canned chicken broth,
    preferably low-salt type
2 cups chopped peeled fresh tomato
    (about 1 pound) or drained
    canned plum tomato
2 bay leaves, crushed
1 cup minced fresh parsley
1 tablespoon minced fresh thyme, or
    1 teaspoon crumbled dried
    thyme
One 4- to 5-pound duck, roasted or
    smoked
1 pound andouille or other smoked
    hot pork sausage, sliced ¼ inch
    thick
Salt
Freshly ground black pepper
About 2 teaspoons Tabasco or other
    red hot pepper sauce
1 teaspoon filé powder
    (if not using okra)
2 cups hot cooked white rice
Minced green onion for garnish

Back in Louisiana, my mother makes fantastic gumbo with wild ducks that my daddy shoots. I have to settle for domestic duck, but the soup is still marvelous. When I have the time to smoke a duck or purchase a smoked duck, this gumbo more nearly approximates the flavor of Mother's game version. Add raw shrimp or oysters, if you wish, about 5 minutes before serving.

Combine the flour and oil in a large, heavy pot, preferably of cast iron, and cook over medium heat, stirring frequently at first then constantly toward the end, until a very dark brown, almost chocolate color, about 35 to 45 minutes.

Add the onions, celery, sweet pepper, and okra, if using, and cook, stirring frequently, until the vegetables are tender, about 15 minutes. Add the garlic and cook about 2 minutes longer. Stir in the stock or broth, tomato, bay leaves, parsley, and thyme. Bring almost to a boil over medium-high heat, then reduce the heat to low and simmer, uncovered, for about 20 minutes.

Remove the meat from the duck, shred or cut the meat into small bite-sized pieces, and stir the leg and thigh meat and the sausage into the soup. Season to taste with salt, pepper, and pepper sauce. Simmer for about 35 minutes.

Add the duck breast meat and simmer to heat through, about 5 minutes. If you did not use okra, remove the pot from the heat and stir in the filé. (Do not add filé if the soup will be chilled first.) Let stand for about 10 minutes, then skim off fat from the surface.

Ladle the gumbo into preheated bowls, top with a scoop of warm rice, and garnish with green onion. Alternatively, pour into a container and refrigerate, uncovered, until cool, then tightly cover and store for as long as 3 days. Skim off and discard any fat; slowly reheat before adding rice and garnish.

Serves 8 as a soup course, or 4 or 5 as a main course.

Sichuan Hot and Sour Soup

Don't skimp on the pepper or vinegar; this soup should be both very hot and very tart. Although components can be readied earlier, cook the soup immediately before serving.

Purchase unusual ingredients from Asian markets.

In a bowl, combine the cornstarch, soy sauce, wine or sherry, ½ teaspoon of the sesame oil, and ginger. Add the pork, toss well, cover, and marinate at room temperature for about 20 minutes, or in the refrigerator for as long as overnight.

In separate bowls, cover the tiger lily buds, cloud ears, and dried mushrooms, if using, with water and soak to soften, at least 25 minutes or as long as overnight. Drain and rinse well. Cut off and discard the hard stem ends from the lily buds and mushrooms and any hard sections from the cloud ears. Slice the lily buds in half lengthwise and thinly slice the mushrooms and cloud ears. If using fresh mushrooms, discard the tough stem ends and thinly slice just before using.

In a soup pot or large saucepan, bring 6 cups of the stock or broth almost to a boil over medium-high heat. Add the marinated pork, reduce the heat to low, and simmer, uncovered, for 5 minutes. Skim off any foam that rises to the top.

Add the lily buds, cloud ears, mushrooms, bamboo shoots, and bean curd to the soup. Cover and simmer for 2 minutes. Stir in the cornstarch mixture and simmer, uncovered, until slightly thickened, about 30 seconds. Add the vinegar and pepper and simmer for about 30 seconds longer. Remove from heat and slowly pour in the egg, stirring gently to distribute. Stir in the remaining 1 teaspoon sesame oil and the green onion. Season to taste with vinegar, salt, and pepper. Quickly ladle the soup into preheated bowls and serve immediately.

Serves 6 as a soup course, or 3 or 4 as a main dish.

1 teaspoon cornstarch
2 tablespoons soy sauce
1 teaspoon Chinese rice wine *(Shaoxing)* or dry sherry
1½ teaspoons Asian-style sesame oil
1 teaspoon minced fresh ginger
½ pound boneless lean pork, thinly sliced, then cut into slivers
About 20 dried tiger lily buds
¼ cup small black cloud ears
6 medium-sized fresh shiitakes or dried black Chinese mushrooms
7 cups Asian-style Poultry Stock (page 10), made with chicken, or canned chicken broth, preferably low-salt type
½ cup julienne-cut bamboo shoots
½ pound fresh firm soybean curd (*dou-fu* or tofu), cut into bite-sized cubes
3 tablespoons cornstarch dissolved in ¼ cup cold water
¼ cup unseasoned Asian-style rice vinegar or distilled white vinegar, or to taste
2 teaspoons freshly ground Sichuan or black pepper, or to taste
1 egg, lightly beaten
About 2 tablespoons thinly sliced green onion, including tops
Salt

Guatemalan Meatball Soup (*Albóndingas*)

MEATBALLS
1 tablespoon vegetable oil
¼ cup finely chopped onion
½ teaspoon minced or pressed garlic
½ pound lean ground beef
1 egg, lightly beaten
¼ cup finely chopped peeled fresh or
    drained canned tomato
1 tablespoon minced fresh mint
1 teaspoon ground cumin
½ teaspoon salt, or to taste
¼ cup fine fresh bread crumbs

3 quarts Meat Stock (page 11), made
    with beef, or canned beef broth
2 cups sliced or diced peeled carrot
    (about 4 medium-sized)
1 pound chayote (about 2 medium-
    sized) or other summer squash,
    peeled, thinly sliced, and
    trimmed into rounds to match
    carrots or diced
½ pound thin-skinned boiling
    potatoes (2 or 3 medium-sized),
    peeled, thinly sliced, and
    trimmed into rounds to match
    carrots or diced
4 or 5 fresh mint sprigs
1 cup small pasta shells, stars, or
    other fanciful soup pasta
Salt
Freshly ground black pepper
Fresh oregano or mint sprigs
    for garnish

This flavorful version of a soup that is served throughout Central America comes from Guatemala via Victoria Flores.

To make the meatballs, heat the oil in a small skillet over medium-high heat. Add the onion and sauté until soft, about 5 minutes. Add the garlic and sauté 1 minute longer. Transfer to a bowl and stir in the remaining ingredients. Working with about 1 teaspoon of the mixture at a time, roll it between the palms of your hands to form balls. Place on a plate, cover loosely, and refrigerate for about 20 minutes before cooking.

In a saucepan, bring 4 cups of the stock or broth to a boil over medium-high heat. Add as many meatballs at a time as will fit comfortably in the pan and cook, skimming off foam as necessary, until done, about 5 minutes. Remove the meatballs with a slotted utensil and set aside; cook the remaining meatballs in the same way. Strain and reserve the cooking liquid for another use.

In a soup pot or large saucepan, combine the remaining 2 quarts stock or broth, carrot, chayote, potatoes, and mint. Bring to a boil over medium-high heat, then reduce the heat to low and simmer, uncovered, until the vegetables are tender, about 25 minutes.

Meanwhile, cook the pasta in a large pot of boiling water until *al dente*. Drain and set aside.

About 5 minutes before the vegetables are done, add the meatballs and pasta to heat through. Season to taste with salt and pepper. Ladle into preheated bowls and garnish with herb sprigs. Alternatively, pour into a container and refrigerate, uncovered, until cool, then tightly cover and store up to 3 days. Slowly reheat before garnishing and serving.

Serves 6 to 8 as a soup course, or 3 or 4 as a main dish.

Nicaraguan Beef and Tripe Soup (*Mondongo*)

Victoria Flores gave me her family's recipe for this wonderful soup.

Wash the tripe under cold running water and pat it dry with paper toweling. Place it in a glass or ceramic bowl, sprinkle with the lime or lemon juice, cover, and refrigerate overnight.

In a soup pot or large, heavy saucepan, heat the oil over medium-high heat. Add the onion and sauté until soft but not browned, about 5 minutes. Add the garlic and sauté 1 minute longer. Add the beef shank and enough water to cover by 2 or 3 inches. Bring to a boil, then reduce the heat to low, cover partially, and simmer for 1 hour. Using a slotted or wire utensil, skim off any scum that rises.

Add the tripe and tomato to the beef and simmer, partially covered, until the beef and tripe are very tender, about 3 hours longer; add water as needed to keep the meat covered.

Remove the beef and tripe from the pot and cool. Cut or shred the beef and cut the tripe into bite-sized pieces; set aside. Discard the beef bones.

Add the plantain to the soup and cook for 10 minutes, then add the yucca and chayote and cook 5 minutes longer. Stir in the cabbage, cilantro, mint, and salt to taste, and cook until all the vegetables are tender, about 15 minutes longer.

Meanwhile, place each of the condiments in separate small bowls for adding at the table.

Discard the herb sprigs from the soup. Ladle the soup into preheated bowls and serve immediately. Alternatively, pour into a container and refrigerate, uncovered, until cool, then tightly cover and store for up to 3 days. Slowly reheat before serving.

Serves 10 as a soup course, or 5 or 6 as a main dish.

5 pounds tripe
½ cup freshly squeezed lemon or lime juice
3 tablespoons vegetable oil
2 cups chopped yellow onion
1 tablespoon minced or pressed garlic
3 pounds meaty beef shank, sawed crosswise into pieces about 2 inches thick
About 3 quarts water
2 cups chopped peeled and seeded fresh tomato (about 1 pound) or drained canned tomato
3 cups sliced slightly green plantains (about 4 medium-sized)
4 cups sliced fresh or thawed frozen yucca (2 bags)
4 cups sliced chayote or other summer squash (about 3 chayote or 1⅓ pounds squash)
1 medium-sized cabbage, cored and sliced into wedges
4 sprigs fresh cilantro (coriander)
4 sprigs fresh mint
Salt

CONDIMENTS
Chopped yellow onion
Sliced radish
Chopped fresh oregano
Chopped fresh cilantro
Lime or lemon wedges
Ground dried hot chile, preferably *ancho* or *pasilla* chile

Fruit & Nut Soups

Applefest Soup

3 tablespoons olive oil
2 cups chopped yellow onion
1 teaspoon minced or pressed garlic
4 cups sliced cored apple,
    peeled if desired
½ teaspoon juniper berry, crushed
½ teaspoon ground cinnamon
¼ teaspoon ground cloves
2 cups chopped flavorful baked ham
    (about 8 ounces)
1 ham bone (optional)
1 tablespoon California-style
    sweet-and-hot-mustard
4 cups Poultry Stock (page 10),
    Vegetable Stock (page 13), or
    canned chicken broth,
    preferably low-salt type
4 cups apple cider
Salt
Freshly ground black pepper
Plain low-fat yogurt or crème fraîche

This soup was created to take to an Applefest picnic, an annual event at the Strybing Arboretum in Golden Gate Park. Like most soups, it is best made ahead and gently reheated before serving.

Choose flavorful, not-too-tart apple varieties such as Macintosh, Red or Golden Delicious, or Gravenstein.

If you wish, top each serving with a piece of cinammon toast cut in the shape of an apple.

In a soup pot or large, heavy saucepan, heat the oil over low heat. Add the onion, cover, and cook, stirring occasionally, until soft and just beginning to color, about 25 minutes. Uncover and increase heat to medium and cook until onion is deep golden and almost caramelized, about 25 minutes longer.

Stir the garlic, apple, juniper berry, cinnamon, cloves, and ham into the onion and sauté about 1 minute. Add the ham bone, if using, mustard, and the stock or broth and cider. Increase the heat to high and bring to a boil. Reduce the heat to low, cover partially, and simmer until the apples are very tender, about 35 minutes. Season to taste with salt and pepper.

Ladle the soup into preheated bowls, top with dollops of yogurt or crème fraîche, and serve immediately. Alternatively, pour into a container and refrigerate, uncovered, until cool, then tightly cover and store for up to 3 days. Slowly reheat before garnishing and serving.

Serves 6 as a soup course, or 3 or 4 as a main dish.

Fresh Fruit Soup

Fruit soup, traditional in Scandinavian countries and the Middle East, can be varied according to which fruits are in season. Serve warm in cold weather or well chilled when the temperature soars. It is frequently served for breakfast, but can begin or end other meals as well.

For a thicker soup, dissolve 2 tablespoons cornstarch in 3 tablespoons cold water, then stir into the simmering soup.

In a soup pot or large saucepan, combine the fruits, sugar, ¼ cup of the lemon juice, and water and bring to a boil over medium-high heat. Reduce the heat to low and simmer, uncovered, until all the fruits are tender, about 15 minutes.

Working in batches, if necessary, transfer the soup to a food processor or blender and purée until fairly smooth. Blend in the remaining ¼ cup lemon juice and the orange juice.

To serve hot, pour into a clean pot and heat over medium-low heat. Ladle into preheated bowls, top with a dollop of yogurt, crème fraîche, or sour cream, sprinkle with cinnamon, if using, and garnish with berries or grapes. Alternatively, pour into a container and refrigerate, uncovered, until cool, then tightly cover and store for up to 3 days. Slowly reheat before garnishing and serving.

To serve cold, pour into a container and refrigerate, uncovered, until cool, then tightly cover and chill for at least 2 hours or as long as 3 days. Ladle into chilled bowls and garnish as for hot soup.

Serves 6 to 8 as a soup course or dessert.

2½ cups peeled, cored, and thinly sliced apples (about 1 pound)
1½ cups peeled, pitted, and thinly sliced peaches (about 1 pound)
1 cup pitted and sliced apricots (about 10 ounces)
1 cup peeled, halved, and pitted plums (about 10 ounces)
1 cup stemmed fresh blueberries or blackberries (about 4 ounces)
1 cup stemmed seedless grapes or pitted cherries (about 6 ounces)
¼ cup sugar, or to taste
½ cup freshly squeezed lemon juice
4 cups water
1 cup freshly squeezed orange juice
Plain yogurt, crème fraîche, or sour cream
Ground cinnamon for sprinkling (optional)
Whole berries or seedless grapes for garnish

Melon Patch Soup

4 cups chopped peeled and seeded ripe
    melon such as cantaloupe,
    crenshaw, or honeydew (one
    kind or an assortment)
2 cups freshly squeezed orange juice
⅓ cup freshly squeezed lemon or
    lime juice
⅓ cup sugar, or to taste
2 cups fruity white wine
3 tablespoons minced fresh mint
Small melon balls for garnish
Scented geranium or mint leaves
    for garnish

A longtime personal favorite combination—melons and mint—creates
an intoxicating hot-weather soup that can begin or end a meal. For
a refreshing look, serve the soup in hollowed-out melons set in a bowl
of crushed ice.

Working in batches, if necessary, combine the melon and citrus juices in a
food processor or blender and purée until fairly smooth. Transfer to a glass
or ceramic bowl and stir in the sugar, wine, and mint. Cover and refrigerate
until chilled, at least 2 hours or as long as overnight.

Ladle into chilled bowls and garnish with melon ball and geranium or mint
leaves.

Serves 6 as a soup course or dessert.

Banana-Coconut Soup

Tropical flavors meld into an unusual soup. Served warm, without the ice cream, it makes a great breakfast or starter for a meal of spicy foods. Chilled and blended with the ice cream, this soup is a cooling snack or dessert.

If coconut milk is unavailable, regular milk may be substituted, or make your own: cover about 2 cups grated fresh or unsweetened dried coconut with 4 cups warm milk and let stand for about 30 minutes. Strain through a colander or a sieve lined with several layers of dampened cheesecloth, squeezing the cloth to release all the liquid.

In a soup pot or large, heavy saucepan, bring the coconut milk to a boil over medium heat. Add the banana, ginger, cinnamon stick, lemon juice, and a pinch of salt to taste. Reduce the heat to low, cover, and simmer until the bananas are very soft, about 10 minutes. Remove the cinnamon stick and let the soup cool slightly.

To serve hot, transfer the warm soup to a food processor or blender, working in batches, if necessary, and purée until smooth. Pour into a clean pot and heat over low heat. (Do not store for later use, as the banana will darken.) Ladle into preheated bowls and garnish with banana slices and toasted coconut.

To serve cold, cool the soup completely, then transfer it to a food processor or blender, working in batches, if necessary. Add the ice cream and purée until smooth. Ladle into chilled bowls and garnish as for hot soup.

Serves 6 as a soup course or dessert.

4 cups canned or thawed frozen
    unsweetened coconut milk
    (available in Asian markets and
    some supermarkets)
4 cups sliced peeled ripe but
    firm banana
2 tablespoons minced peeled
    fresh ginger root
1 cinnamon stick
1 tablespoon freshly squeezed
    lemon juice
Salt
Banana slices for garnish
    (cut just before serving)
Toasted shredded coconut
    for garnish
1 pint rich coconut or banana
    ice cream (optional)

Sparkling Berry Soup

6 cups stemmed ripe berries such as
    strawberries, raspberries, or
    blackberries (one kind or
    an assortment)
1 cup freshly squeezed orange juice
¼ cup freshly squeezed lemon juice
½ cup sugar, or to taste
2 cups Asti Spumante, Champagne,
    or other sparkling wine
Berry sorbet, frozen vanilla yogurt,
    or rich vanilla ice cream
Whole fresh berries for garnish
Pesticide-free, non-toxic flowers such
    as borage, forget-me-nots,
    violas, or violets for garnish
    (optional)

Serve as a soup course at the beginning of a meal, as an interlude between courses, or as a light dessert.

Working in batches, if necessary, combine the berries and citrus juices in a food processor or blender and purée until fairly smooth.

Transfer to a glass or ceramic bowl and stir in the sugar and sparkling wine. Cover and refrigerate until chilled, at least 2 hours or as long as overnight.

Ladle into chilled bowls, top with a small scoop of sorbet, frozen yogurt, or ice cream, and garnish with berries and flowers, if using.

Serves 6 as a soup course or dessert.

Prune Soup with Cardamom Cream

Serve this exotic soup at breakfast or brunch, to start a Middle Eastern meal, or as a light dessert.

In a large saucepan over medium-high heat, combine the prunes, prune juice, cinnamon sticks, and cloves and bring to a boil. Reduce the heat to low and simmer, uncovered, until the prunes are plumped and very tender, about 15 minutes. Cool the soup slightly, then discard the spices.

Working in batches, if necessary, transfer the soup to a food processor or blender and purée until smooth. Stir in the port and lemon juice. If serving the soup hot, pour into a clean pot; if serving cold, pour into a container.

To toast the pine nuts, place them in a small dry skillet over medium heat and cook, stirring frequently, until lightly toasted, about 5 minutes. Pour onto a plate and set aside to cool.

Shortly before serving, pour the cream into a chilled bowl and beat with a wire whisk or electric hand mixer until it just begins to thicken. Add the cardamom and continue whipping until the cream just holds its shape. Set aside.

To serve hot, heat the soup over medium-low heat. Ladle into preheated soup bowls, top with whipped cream, and quickly draw the tip of a wooden skewer or a small sharp knife through the cream to form a pattern on the soup. Sprinkle with pine nuts and serve immediately.

To serve cold, cover, and chill for at least 2 hours or up to 3 days. Ladle into chilled bowls and garnish as for hot soup.

Serves 6 as a soup course or dessert.

About 40 dried pitted prunes
1 quart prune juice
2 cinnamon sticks
About 6 whole cloves
½ cup port wine
2 tablespoons freshly squeezed
    lemon juice, or to taste
½ cup pine nuts
½ cup very cold heavy (whipping)
    cream
1 tablespoon ground cardamom, or
    to taste

Pistachio-Avocado Soup

Essence of the fabled California sunshine captured in a bowl. Almonds can be substituted for the pistachios.

Combine the pistachios, garlic, and 1½ cups of the stock or broth in a saucepan and cook over medium heat until the nuts are tender and most of the liquid evaporates, about 10 minutes. Remove from heat and cool slightly.

Purée the avocados in a food processor or blender. Add the cooked pistachio mixture, remaining 1 cup stock or broth, and lime juice. Purée until smooth, then blend in the cream and season to taste with salt and pepper.

To serve hot, transfer the soup to a saucepan and heat over medium-low heat until heated through; do not allow to boil. Ladle into preheated bowls, garnish with avocado cubes, chopped pistachios, and a flower, if using, and serve immediately. Alternatively, pour into a container and refrigerate, uncovered, until cool, then tightly cover and store up to 3 days. Slowly reheat before serving; do not boil.

To serve cold, pour into a container and refrigerate, uncovered, until cool, then tightly cover and chill for at least 2 hours or as long as 3 days. Ladle into chilled bowls and garnish as for hot soup.

Serves 6 as a soup course, or 4 as a main dish.

1 cup shelled pistachios
½ teaspoon minced or pressed garlic
2½ cups Poultry Stock (page 10) or canned chicken broth, preferably low-salt type
2 large ripe avocados, peeled and seeded
1½ teaspoons freshly squeezed lime juice
2 cups heavy (whipping) cream
Salt
Freshly ground white pepper
Avocado cubes tossed in freshly squeezed lime juice for garnish
Chopped pistachios for garnish
Pesticide-free, non-toxic flowers such as geraniums for garnish (optional)

Peanutty Yam Soup

Two southern favorites—peanut butter and yams (the richer-hued and sweetest varieties of sweet potatoes)—teamed to create a smooth rich soup that makes a great starter, snack, or a simple meal.

In a soup pot or large heavy saucepan, melt the butter over medium heat. Add the onion, celery, and yams and sauté until the onion and celery are soft but not browned, about 5 minutes. Add the stock or broth and bring to a boil, then reduce the heat to low, cover, and simmer until the yams are very tender, about 30 minutes. Remove from heat and cool slightly.

Working in batches, if necessary, transfer the soup to a food processor or blender. Add the peanut butter and purée until smooth. Season to taste with salt and pepper.

To serve hot, transfer to a clean saucepan and heat over low heat; do not boil. Ladle into preheated bowls, sprinkle with chopped peanuts, and serve immediately. Alternatively, pour into a container and refrigerate until cool, then tightly cover and store for up to 3 days. Slowly reheat before garnishing and serving; do not boil.

To serve cold, pour into a container and refrigerate, uncovered, until cool, then tightly cover and chill for at least 2 hours or as long as 3 days. Remove from the refrigerator about 25 minutes before serving. Ladle into chilled bowls and garnish as for hot soup.

Serves 6 to 8 as a soup course, or 3 or 4 as a main dish.

¼ cup (½ stick) unsalted butter
½ cup chopped yellow onion
½ cup chopped celery
6 cups peeled and sliced yam
    (about 2 pounds)
2 quarts Poultry Stock (page 10) or
    canned chicken broth,
    preferably low-salt type
1¼ cups smooth peanut butter
Salt
Freshly ground black pepper
Chopped roasted peanuts for garnish

Toasted Pecan Soup

2¼ cups shelled pecans
2 tablespoons unsalted butter
¼ cup chopped shallot
1 cup chopped leek,
    white portion only
½ cup chopped fennel or celery
¼ cup packed light brown sugar
1 teaspoon ground cinnamon
1 tablespoon minced fresh thyme, or
    1 teaspoon crumbled dried
    thyme
1 bay leaf
6 cups Poultry Stock (page 10) or
    canned chicken broth,
    preferably low-salt type
Salt
Freshly ground white pepper
¾ cup heavy (whipping) cream
1 tablespoon Worcestershire sauce
2 tablespoons bourbon or sherry

Worth every calorie-laden spoonful to a pecan lover like me! Also try this savory soup with cashews, hazelnuts, macadamias, or other nuts.

Preheat an oven to 350° F.

Spread the pecans in an ovenproof pan and toast in the oven, stirring frequently, until lightly browned and fragrant, about 15 minutes. Chop coarsely and set aside.

In a soup pot or large, heavy saucepan, melt the butter over low heat. Add the shallot, leek, and fennel or celery and cook, stirring frequently, until tender, about 10 minutes.

Add 2 cups of the toasted pecans (reserve the rest for garnish), brown sugar, cinnamon, thyme, and bay leaf and cook, stirring frequently, for about 5 minutes. Stir in the stock or broth and bring almost to a boil over medium heat. Season to taste with salt and pepper. Reduce the heat to low and simmer, uncovered, until the pecans are very tender, about 2 hours. Discard the bay leaf.

Working in batches, if necessary, transfer the soup to a food processor or blender and purée until smooth.

Pour the soup into a clean pot and bring to a boil over high heat. Reduce the heat to low, stir in the cream, Worcestershire, and bourbon or sherry and simmer until the alcohol evaporates, about 2 minutes.

To serve hot, ladle into preheated soup bowls and garnish with the reserved toasted pecans. Alternatively, pour into a container and refrigerate, uncovered, until cool, then tightly cover and store for up to 3 days. Slowly reheat before garnishing and serving; do not boil.

To serve cold, pour into a container and refrigerate, uncovered, until cool, then tightly cover and chill for at least 2 hours or as long as 3 days. Remove from the refrigerator about 25 minutes before serving. Ladle into chilled bowls and garnish.

Serves 6 to 8 as a soup course, or 3 or 4 as a main dish.

Hazelnut-Chocolate Soup

4 cups light cream or half-and-half
6 ounces semisweet or bittersweet
    chocolate
½ cup sugar
4 egg yolks, at room temperature
⅓ cup crème de cacao
3 tablespoons Frangelico
    (hazelnut liqueur)
½ cup heavy (whipping) cream,
    lightly whipped
½ cup chopped toasted hazelnuts

Serve this unexpected treat as a brunch opener or a dessert soup. For an even more opulent presentation, float a heart-shaped sugar cookie on top of each serving.

In a saucepan, combine the light cream or half-and-half, chocolate, and sugar and place over medium-low heat, stirring frequently, until the chocolate melts.

Beat the egg yolks in a small bowl, then whisk in about ½ cup of the hot chocolate mixture. Whisk the egg mixture into the soup and simmer, stirring frequently, until the soup thickens slightly, about 5 minutes. Remove from heat and stir in the liqueurs.

To serve hot, ladle into warmed bowls, add a dollop of whipped cream, sprinkle with the hazelnuts, and serve immediately. Alternatively, pour into a container, tightly cover, and refrigerate for up to 5 days. Slowly reheat before garnishing and serving.

To serve cold, pour into a container, tightly cover, and refrigerate until chilled, at least 2 hours or as long as 5 days. Remove from the refrigerator about 20 minutes before serving. Ladle into chilled bowls and garnish as for hot soup.

Serves 6 as a brunch soup course or dessert.

Index

Recipe Index

Index to Soup Recipes in Other James McNair Cookbooks

ACKNOWLEDGMENTS

Hand-marbled papers used as backgrounds were made by the following artists and reproduced with their permission:

Galen Berry, Walnut Creek, California: pages 4, 14-15, 17, 29, 32, 36, 40, 43, 50-51, 53, 63, 66, 69, 72-73, 75, 76, 79, 83, 84, 86, and 93.

Dana and Ingrid Draper of Moth Marblers, Sausalito, California: pages 19, 25, 34, 45, 48, 58, 60, 65, 70, 88, and 91.

Trudy Lombard, Lyme, Connecticut: cover, pages 20, 26, 47, 54, and 80.

Imported papers on pages 22, 31, 39, and 57 are from Elicia's Papers, Berkeley, California.

Silver ladles on pages 14, 50, and 72 are from Tiffany and Company.

Izabel Lam spoons on pages 43 and 76 are from Mottura, Los Angeles.

To Chronicle Books for their continued great work on my behalf. Special thanks this time to Julie Noyes in the art department, who always does a terrific job coordinating the printing of my books.

To Cleve Gallat and Charles Sublett of CTA Graphics for another excellent job of typesetting and mechanicals.

To Ellen Berger-Quan, my assistant, for her amazing energy and efficiency in the office, out shopping, in the test kitchen, and in the studio.

To Patricia Brabant, my photographer, for another spectacular job behind the lenses. And to M. J. Murphy, photography assistant, for keeping us on track in the photo studios, both in San Francisco and at Lake Tahoe.

To Butterfield and Butterfield, Christine High, Kristi Spence, Burt Tessler, and Jim Wentworth for the loan of soup spoons.

To my family and friends who always provide impetus for all my work.

To Addie Prey, Buster Booroo, Joshua J. Chew, Michael T. Wigglebutt, and Dweasel Pickle, my loyal companions, who are especially fond of soup stock.

To Lin Cotton, my partner, for his constant encouragement and prodding towards greater achievements.